LET'S G

O DANCING

Elizabeth Romain and Flick Colby

CONTENTS

Foreword	9
Introduction	10
BALLROOM DANCING	14
The Social Foxtrot	18
Quarter Turns	20
Reverse Rock Turn	22
Natural Rock Turn	23
Promenade Chassé	24
Exit to Side Step	26
Side Step	27
The Waltz	30
Natural Turn and Right Foot Closed Change	32
Reverse Turn and Left Foot Closed Change	34
Hesitation Change	36
Outside Change	38
Natural Spin Turn	40
The Quickstep	44
Quarter Turn to Right, Progressive Chassé and Forward Lock	46
Natural Turn	50
Natural Hesitation Turn to Chassé Reverse Turn with Progressive Chassé ending	52
The Tango	56
Closed Promenade	58
Two Walks and Progressive Link	59
Walk into Rock Turn	60
Open Reverse Turn	62
Four Step	64
Natural Promenade Turn	65
LATIN AMERICAN DANCING	68
The Cha Cha Cha	70
Basic Movement	72
Time Steps	74
Lady's Turn to Right under the Arms	76
Spot Turns	78
New York	80
The Jive	84
Fallaway Rock	86
Change of Places from Right to Left	88
Change of Places from Left to Right	90
Link Rock	92
American Spin	94
The Samba	98
Reverse Basic Movement	100
Whisks	102
Walks in Promenade Position	104
Reverse Turn	106
Volta Movements	108
The Rumba	112
Basic Movement	114
Fan	116
Alemana	118
Hand to Hand and Spot Turn	120
The Paso Doble	126
Chassé to Right	128
Sur Place	129
Forward Basic Movement	129
Separation	130
Promenade Link	131
Medal Tests and Competitions	134
DISCO DANCING	138
Rock and Roll: the Lindyhop	142
Rock and Roll variations	143
The Stroll	146
The Twist, the Shimmy	148
The Frug, the Jerk, the Monkey, the Hitchhiker	150
The Pony, the Swim	152
The Bump	153
The Hustle	154

Photograph: Malcolm Robertson

The publishers are grateful to the following people
for their help in producing this book:
Bryan Anthony
Walter Laird of the Ballroom Dancing Federation
For dancing in the photographic sessions:
Ballroom Greg Smith and Marie Alleyn
and *Disco* Floyd Pearce and Patti Hammond

First published 1979 by
Octopus Books Limited
59 Grosvenor Street
London W1

ISBN 0 7064 0965 5

D. L. To-690-79

Printed in Spain by Artes Gráficas Toledo, S. A.

Foreword

Dancing today is enjoying its greatest popularity of all time. This is undoubtedly due to the phenomenon called the Hustle, the dance that has brought people together again on the dance floor. The Hustle is what is referred to as 'contact disco'. It's a contact dance that originated in the discothèques, and the young people of today have suddenly become aware of the fascinating world of contact dancing.

Because of the fun and enjoyment they derived from dancing the Hustle, it was inevitable that these new aficionados of dance would awaken to the whole spectrum of ballroom and Latin American dancing. In our studio we've found that many young (and also not so young) people who have come in to learn the Hustle then start to ask about the Jitterbug (also known as the Lindy, Jive, Swing etc.) the Cha Cha Cha and other dances such as the Tango and, of course, the Waltz. Our beginners classes in ballroom dancing are usually filled and have a waiting list for the next class.

People are suddenly aware of the strong social aspects of ballroom dancing. It is very fashionable again to dance the Waltz at weddings. It's 'in' to go to dinner dances, banquets and parties where the major emphasis is on dancing. The Hustle dancer who can do a lively Jive and a rhythmic Cha Cha Cha is now the hit of parties and more and more people want to take part in this exciting social pastime.

Because of the increased interest in learning all the dances, it is only logical that the need arises for a simple straightforward book describing the basic steps for the various ballroom and Latin dances. To meet these needs a book on social ballroom dancing must be clear enough to be readily understood by the beginner. It must cover the dances most popular today and, although simple, it should have enough variety in each dance to make it interesting and exciting to learn.

'Let's Go Dancing' is just such a book. I find its basic and accurate descriptions very easy to understand. The step patterns selected offer good variety and include some exciting movements even at a beginner's level. The descriptions of the man's and lady's steps are simple and precise, and the section at the end of each dance suggesting ways to link the steps together should prove extremely helpful especially to the new dancer. Also included are brief but informative sections on rhythm and timing, poise and hold, and very valuable sections on how to improve the dances as you progress beyond the basic level.

Many disco dancers are now interested in all the dances and want to learn them. This book should provide an exciting introduction to the most popular social dances and will undoubtedly prove to be a valuable tool in the hands of both the teacher and student.

Dennis Rogers
President of US Imperial Society of Teachers of Dancing

INTRODUCTION

Let's go dancing! What do these words mean to you? Soft lights, sweet music? An elegant, graceful you gliding around the floor in the arms of the one you love? A happy social evening with friends? The confidence that you can dance and that others will want to dance with you? Or do you picture agonizing hours of sitting in a corner trying to look as if you like being alone? Do you see yourself stumbling around the floor apologizing to an unhappy partner, desperately trying to make your left foot do what your right foot should have done?

Possibly there have been times when you have stood on the edge of a dance floor watching with envy the obvious enjoyment of the dancers and wishing with all your heart that you could summon up enough courage to join them. Perhaps they are dancing a graceful Waltz or exhilarating Samba, or gyrating rhythmically to the disco music of today. . . . Yet, with a little practice and perseverance you could join them.

Our natural instinct tells us that we want to express rhythm. The tiniest tot will bob up and down to a jolly tune, and the most senior citizen will tap a foot to a pulsating beat. Dancing is for everyone, young and old, rich and poor. It provides great mental relaxation and as much physical exercise as desired. If you can walk, you can dance – so start right now.

The ballroom section of this book deals with the dances that are known as 'the standard four', namely Foxtrot, Waltz, Quickstep and Tango. The Foxtrot proper is an elegant dance, the classic of the ballroom; but to do it justice, the dancers need a great deal of space, and it is not very practicable to dance it on small, crowded floors. In these conditions, most people dance the Social Foxtrot, which is sometimes known as 'Crush' or 'Rhythm' dancing. It is the Social Foxtrot, not the Foxtrot proper, that is described in this book, and it appears first as it is the easiest dance to master and the most useful for a beginner.

At most dances the band will play Foxtrot, Waltz and Quickstep more frequently than Tango, and there will be more opportunity to dance Cha Cha Cha, Jive and Samba than Rumba and Paso Doble. The last five dances are known as the Latin American standard five and are described in the Latin American section. In describing the dances, the book follows this order of popularity.

Young people of today spend a great deal of time in crowded discos and because there isn't really room to move around the floor or use intricate step patterns they use their bodies and arms in a very rhythmic way, inspired by the modern pop music of this era. A further section of the book is devoted to disco dancing and to Rock and Roll.

Left and previous page : Glenn and Lynette Boyce from Bournemouth dancing at the Star Professional Ballroom Championship in 1979.

Now, what equipment will you need? First, music on discs or tapes. Many bands record strict-tempo dance music, and your local music dealer should be able to obtain this for you.

Next, the right dress. This of course will be dictated both by fashion and by the type of venue or function you are attending. Obviously you would not dream of arriving at a disco in formal evening attire any more than you would attend a dinner and dance at a hotel in jeans! There are always ways and means of finding out what everyone else will be wearing, but here are some golden rules for your own comfort.

Always choose clothes that are cool – it can get uncomfortably warm in crowded places, especially when you are dancing. You will feel happier in something loose rather than clothes that restrict your movement and the use of your arms.

Shoes, of course, are most important. They need to be light and flexible, at the same time giving your feet the necessary support. Thick soles and clumpy heels will not help your dancing or enhance your popularity if you tread on your partner's toes! And do make sure they are the right size. You will not enjoy dancing if your feet hurt.

As you progress, you will probably want to invest in a pair of shoes especially made for dancing. These have soles which minimize skidding on a slippery floor and help you feel secure and confident. Dance magazines and papers provide the names of many manufacturers who make shoes with styles and heel heights to suit all tastes.

Now to the dance floor itself. This can be rectangular, square, circular, oval, small or large, but whatever its shape or size it is necessary to understand the correct method of progressing around the floor.

To do this, imagine you are driving a car in a country where cars are driven on the right-hand side of the road. On your right are the pavement and buildings. They are the equivalent of the wall of the dance floor. On your left is the centre of the road. This is the centre of the floor. You must drive straight down the road. This is the line of dance.

Imagine there is a central barrier in the road. You must not cross this barrier or you will collide with the oncoming traffic. Similarly, on the dance floor, the rule is KEEP RIGHT.

Stand facing the line of dance and turn 45 degrees to the right. You are now facing diagonally to the wall.

Face the line of dance again and turn 45 degrees to the left. You are now facing diagonally to the centre.

Study diagram (i) until you understand all the directions.

In partnership dancing, the man is always the 'driver', so he needs a thorough understanding of his directions in relation to the ballroom. The lady will find them equally important when learning the figures on her own, but when she is dancing with a partner she must follow the direction of his 'steering'.

In some Latin American dances, the partners do not dance around the floor but stay in one place. However, in most of the instructions for these dances, directions are still given to make the figures easier to learn.

Now you must learn the instructions given for the position of the feet in dancing. To do this imagine the face of a big clock on the floor. Stand in the centre of the clock with your feet together, facing 12 o'clock.

Move your right foot towards 12 o'clock. This is 'right foot forward'. Return your foot to the starting position. Move it sideways towards three o'clock. This is 'right foot to the side'. Again return it to the starting position. Move it towards half past one. This is 'right foot diagonally forward'.

Have you got the idea? Good. Now look at diagram (ii) and try all the positions – first with your right foot, then with your left – until you are thoroughly familiar with them all.

Now you are almost ready to read the instructions and to try your first steps. Before you start, here are a few helpful hints.

1. Always read the introduction to each section or individual dance thoroughly.

2. Learn the step pattern on your own. Practise slowly and carefully until you feel ready to try it to music. If you own a record- or cassette-player with a variable speed control, slow down the music to start with, gradually speeding it up to the correct tempo as you become more confident.

3. When you have mastered two or three figures, try to put them together. At the end of each dance you will find guidance on how to do this. As you gain confidence and experience, you will discover the figures that follow others quite naturally and can have great fun in varying the patterns. The man is the boss in creating these patterns, even in these days of Women's Lib! It is his responsibility to make the decisions, and his partner's responsibility to follow. Both roles, although different, are equally important.

4. Try to stand and think 'tall' when you are dancing. Nothing looks worse than rounded shoulders and a seat sticking out. Do not look at your feet – it does not help them at all! Correct stance and head carriage will assist your balance, help your dancing and make you look and feel good.

5. Do not worry if things go wrong. You will gradually improve with practice.

6. It is not difficult to become a competent ballroom dancer. You will obtain more pleasure from doing a few simple steps well than many intricate figures badly.

As you will see, the foot-plans for each figure in a dance usually run from right to left. When there is more than one figure on a double page, learn the figure on the right-hand page first. Every foot-plan box has a number at the bottom left-hand corner. This is the step number. At the bottom right-hand corner there is a word (quick, slow, one, a, two etc.) indicating the beat count for the step.

This book will introduce you to the pleasures of dancing, and help you improve your dancing if you have already made a start. It cannot take the place of a good teacher, so if you want to develop your skills or learn more dances and figures take yourself off to your nearest dancing school. Now turn the pages and take your first steps into a whole new world. Let's go dancing!

i

ii

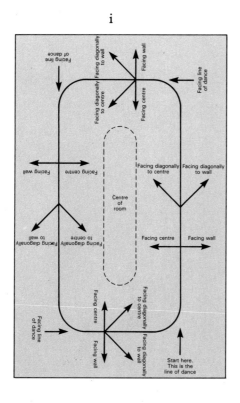

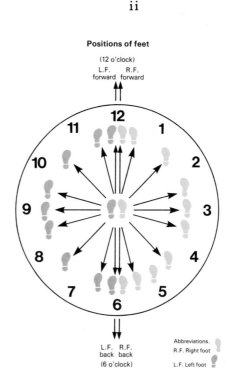

BALLROOM DANCING

Ballroom dancing is based on natural walking steps. To do these steps comfortably with a partner, and to achieve the free, flowing movement which is so much a part of dancing, it is very important to poise the body correctly.

First practise alone. Stand up straight with your feet closed, toes together, heels together, knees fairly straight but not rigid. Feel that your shoulders are directly over your hips and that your hips are directly over your feet. Take a deep breath. This will slightly brace your diaphragm. Try to keep this position as you breathe out and relax your shoulders.

Take your weight fully on to the right foot and incline your body weight very slightly forward, retaining the body position you have just achieved.

Now take a step forward with your left foot. If your poise and weight distribution are correct the left foot will start to move forward with the ball of the foot lightly skimming the floor. Put your weight on to the left foot, heel first, like a normal walking step. The right heel should leave the floor quite naturally if your body weight is over your left foot. Just to check, look down. If you cannot see your left foot your weight is correct. If you *can* see the left foot, move your body weight forward until it is hidden. Do not forget to look up again – because when you are actually dancing you should never look down.

Now swing the right foot past the left foot as if you are walking, and continue moving it in the same way as you moved the left foot. Always feel the body starting to move forward just before the foot. If your foot goes first you will look as if you are starting to sit down.

Next practise walking backwards. This is a little more difficult, as it is a much less natural movement. Stand with your feet together in the same upright position as before. Take your weight fully on to the left foot and move your right foot back, first with the ball of the foot skimming the floor then stretching the foot to the toe. Imagine that you are trying to show most of the sole of your shoe to someone behind you.

At the full length of the step lower the heel slightly towards the floor and let your left toe leave the floor. Your weight is now centralized between the ball of the back foot and the heel of the front foot.

Start to move the left foot back towards the right foot, allowing the ball of the left foot to touch the floor again. At the same time lower the right heel very gradually. Swing the left foot past the right foot and continue to walk back with the left foot in the same way. To ensure that your body weight does not fall back, try not to lower the right heel fully to the floor until the left foot is passing it. This requires quite a lot of practice. It is a good idea to steady yourself at first by walking beside a wall, lightly touching the wall with your hand to help you keep your balance.

Now try four walks forward and four back – or more, if room permits. It does not matter which foot starts first. Keep the feet straight, letting the insides touch each other lightly as they pass. As one foot passes the other, the knees should be slightly flexed, but at the full extent of the step they should be straight – though not stiff.

If you are lucky enough to have a partner with whom to practise, you are now ready to try the walks together. Face each other, a little apart, and place your hands lightly on each other's shoulders. The man should do four forward walks while the lady goes back, then reverse the procedure so that he goes back and the lady forward. Keep practising this until it becomes quite easy.

You are now ready to take up your ballroom hold as shown in the diagrams. As the lady faces the man, she must always be slightly to his right – because it is impossible for the partners to move forward or backward freely if their feet are exactly opposite.

Try the forward and backward walks in ballroom hold. This will be a little more difficult than before, but keep trying until you are moving comfortably and smoothly together. It will be easier if you stand slightly apart at the beginning.

Always look over your partner's right shoulder so that you can see where you are going. Try to keep your body weight forward towards your partner and never let it drop back over your heels, whether moving forward or backward.

In leading and following there are some important points to bear in mind.

1. In some dances you may start with either foot. The man must make the decision, and this will usually depend on the figure he wants to dance. When in the dance position, the man must take his weight very definitely on to his right foot if he wishes to start with his left foot. The lady should feel the shifting of weight quite easily and respond accordingly by taking her weight on to the left foot. It is the man's responsibility not to start dancing until he feels his partner is ready with her weight on the correct foot.

2. The man should first master his steps alone. When he knows them quite thoroughly, the lady should have no difficulty in following him if the hold and

Ballroom hold : man's back view

Ballroom hold : lady's back view

Ballroom hold : side view

poise are correct and the man is dancing his steps with confidence.

3. The lady must remember that correct poise will keep her up to her partner and make her light and easy to lead. She should try to incline her head and shoulders slightly back – but only slightly as otherwise she will tend to drop her weight back over her heels and pull away from her partner. This will make her heavy to dance with and difficult to lead.

4. The lady should also remember not to bear down on her partner with her arms. He will not enjoy dragging or pushing her around the floor!

5. The man must not grasp his partner like a vice. She will enjoy her dancing far more if she can breathe! He should not allow the fingers of his right hand to spread out on the lady's back, as this looks ugly. He should also keep his left arm quite still and not try to lead the lady by moving it up and down or forward or backward.

6. Never be hesitant in your movements, or your partner will find it difficult to react correctly.

7. Never spreadeagle your feet to avoid stepping on your partner when moving forward. If your poise and hold are correct and you are moving forward confidently, the need to do this should never arise.

Well, you are now ready to learn your first ballroom dance. Just one final word before you begin. When you are learning, do not try to take long steps. It is much easier to dance in a controlled and balanced way if you take normal-length steps. As you gain experience, you can lengthen your steps if space permits, but always show consideration for others by shortening them when the floor is small and crowded with other dancers.

Promenade Position

Tango hold : man's back view

Promenade Position : man's back view showing position of lady's left hand throughout tango

THE SOCIAL FOXTROT

The Social Foxtrot can be danced in a small space and is easy to learn. It is certainly most useful for the beginner as it can be danced to almost any music other than waltz music. The hold is described and illustrated on page 16 – but when the floor is crowded, it is considerate to the other dancers to keep the hold more compact than the illustration shows. The tempo of the Foxtrot music is usually about 32 bars a minute, but as you become familiar with the steps you will find it easy to dance them to faster music, such as that of a Quickstep. In Foxtrot music each bar has four beats. Listen carefully and you will hear a steady 'One, Two, Three, Four'. A slow step takes two beats, and a quick step takes one beat. Try walking to the music counting two numbers for each step – 'One, Two', 'Three, Four' .... You are doing slow steps. Now walk to the music counting one number only for each step – 'One'. 'Two', 'Three', 'Four' .... You are doing quick steps. In the figures described you will always do two slow steps followed by two quick steps, like this: Slow, Slow, Quick, Quick; Slow, Slow, Quick, Quick. This rhythm will never change. The man will start every figure with his left foot and the lady with her right foot.

Try the following exercise.

Man's steps

Two slow steps: left foot forward, right foot forward. Say 'Slow, Slow'. Two quick steps: left foot to the side, close the right foot to it. Say 'Quick, Quick'. Two slow steps: left foot back, right foot back. Say 'Slow, Slow'. Two quick steps: left foot to the side, close the right foot to it. Say 'Quick, Quick'.

Lady's steps

Two slow steps: right foot back, left foot back. Say 'Slow, Slow'. Two quick steps: right foot to the side, close the left foot to it. Say 'Quick, Quick'. Two slow steps: right foot forward, left foot forward. Say 'Slow, Slow'. Two quick steps: right foot to the side, close the left foot to it. Say 'Quick, Quick'.

Now try this exercise to music, and when you feel you can do it with ease you are ready to learn the Quarter Turns.

Quarter Turns

To make a Quarter Turn, you simply do the four basic steps you have already learned, but turning a quarter to the right or left as you step to the side and close. Start off with a Quarter Turn to the Right, then one to the Left, and repeat this over and over again.

QUARTER TURN TO LEFT

Step 2

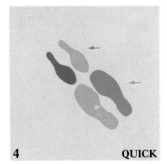 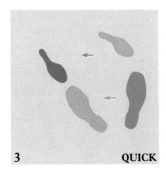 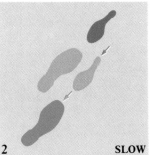 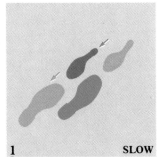

4 QUICK	3 QUICK	2 SLOW	1 SLOW

Man's steps
Start with the back diagonal to the centre.
1 LF back (on toe, then lower to heel).

4 Close RF to LF, facing diagonally to the wall (foot flat).

3 Still turning to the left, LF to the side, and pointing diagonally to the wall (small step, foot flat).

2 RF back, starting to turn to the left (on toe, then lower to heel).

Lady's steps
Start by facing diagonally to the centre.
1 RF forward (heel first).

4 Close LF to RF (foot flat).

3 Still turning to the left, RF to the side, with the back diagonal to the wall (foot flat).

2 LF forward, starting to turn to the left (heel first).

Start here

QUARTER TURN TO RIGHT

Step 4

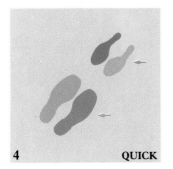 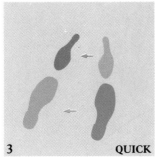 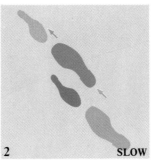 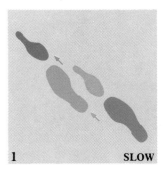

| 4 QUICK | 3 QUICK | 2 SLOW | 1 SLOW |

4 Close RF to LF (foot flat).

3 Still turning to the right, LF to the side, backing diagonally to the centre (foot flat).

2 RF forward, starting to turn to the right (heel first).

Man's steps
Start by facing diagonally to the wall.
1 LF forward (heel first).

4 Close LF to RF, facing diagonally to the centre (foot flat).

3 Still turning to the right, RF to the side and pointing diagonally to the centre (small step, foot flat).

2 LF back, starting to turn to the right (on toe, then lower to heel).

Lady's steps
Start with the back diagonal to the wall.
1 RF back (on toe, then lower to heel).

21

Reverse Rock Turn

You will be ready to dance this figure after the Quarter Turn to Left. As in the Natural Rock Turn you turn a quarter, but this time to the left. Dance the figure four times to complete a full turn. Follow with the Quarter Turn to Right.

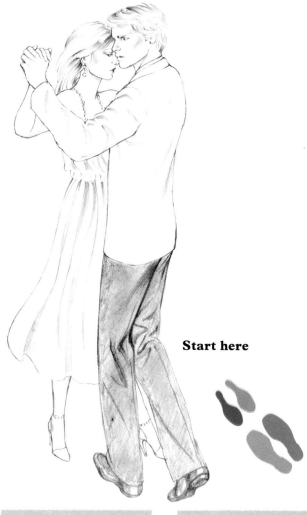

Start here

Step 1

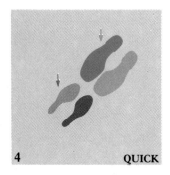

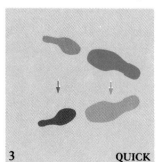

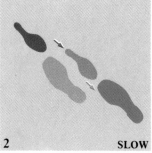

4   QUICK   **3**   QUICK   **2**   SLOW   **1**   SLOW

4 Close RF to LF, facing diagonally to the centre (foot flat).

3 Still turning to the left, LF to the side, and pointing diagonally to the centre (small step, foot flat).

2 Replace weight back to RF, starting to turn to the left (on toe, then lower to heel).

Man's steps
Start by facing diagonally to the wall.
1 LF forward (heel first).

4 Close LF to RF (foot flat).

3 Still turning to the left, RF to the side, backing diagonally to the centre (foot flat).

2 Replace weight forward to LF, starting to turn to the left (heel first).

Lady's steps
Start with the back diagonal to the wall.
1 RF back (on toe, then lower to heel).

Natural Rock Turn

First dance the Quarter Turn to Right. You are now in position to dance the Natural Rock Turn. A Quarter Turn to the Right is made in this figure so dancing it four times in succession brings you back to your starting position. Follow with the Quarter Turn to Left.

Start here

Step 1

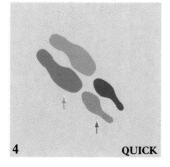

4   QUICK

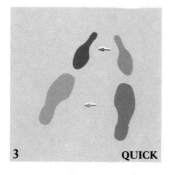

3   QUICK

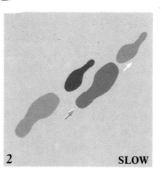

2   SLOW

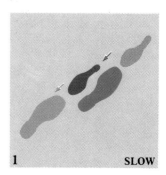

1   SLOW

4 Close RF to LF (foot flat).

3 Still turning to the right, LF to the side, backing diagonally to the wall, (foot flat).

2 Replace weight forward to RF, starting to turn to the right (heel first).

Man's steps
Start with the back diagonal to the centre.
1 LF back (on toe, then lower to heel).

4 Close LF to RF, facing diagonally to the wall (foot flat).

3 Still turning to the right, RF to the side and pointing diagonally to the wall (small step, foot flat).

2 Replace weight back to LF starting to turn to the right (on toe, then lower to heel).

Lady's steps
Start by facing diagonally to the centre.
1 RF forward (heel first).

Promenade Chassé

First dance the Quarter Turn to Right. The man then does his normal Quarter Turn to Left but the lady does not turn with him. To prevent the lady turning at the end of his second step, the man must exert a little pressure on the lady's back through the heel of his hand.

You will now be in the Promenade Position as illustrated on page 17.

The Promenade Chassé progresses along the line of dance in Promenade Position. You may repeat the figure two or three times. To finish, the man makes a Quarter Turn to Right to face the lady as he dances steps 3 and 4. The lady does not turn.

Follow with the Quarter Turn to Left.

PROMENADE CHASSÉ

Step 2

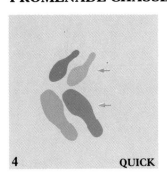 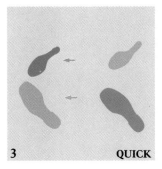 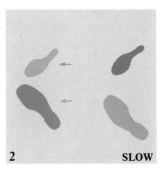 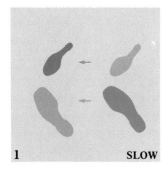

| 4 QUICK | 3 QUICK | 2 SLOW | 1 SLOW |

Man's steps

4 Close RF to LF in Promenade Position (foot flat).

3 LF to the side in Promenade Position (foot flat).

2 RF forward and across the LF in Promenade Position (heel first).

1 LF to the side in Promenade Position (heel first).

Lady's steps

4 Close LF to RF in Promenade Position (foot flat).

3 RF to the side in Promenade Position (foot flat).

2 LF forward and across the RF in Promenade Position (heel first).

1 RF to the side in Promenade Position (heel first).

Step 4

Start here

ENTRY — QUARTER TURN TO LEFT TO PROMENADE POSITION

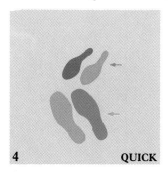

4   QUICK

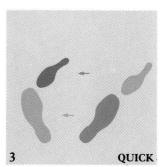

3   QUICK

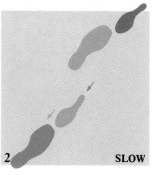

2   SLOW

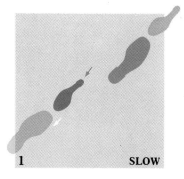

1   SLOW

4 Close RF to LF in Promenade Position, facing diagonally to the wall (foot flat).

4 Close LF to RF (foot flat).

3 Still turning to the left, LF to the side, and pointing diagonally to the wall in Promenade Position (small step, foot flat).

3 RF to the side in Promenade Position, still facing diagonally to the centre (foot flat).

2 RF back, starting to turn to the left (on toe, then lower to heel).

2 LF forward (heel first).

Man's steps
Start with the back diagonal to the centre.
1 LF back (on toe, then lower to heel).

Lady's steps
Start by facing diagonally to the centre.
1 RF forward (heel first).

25

Exit to Side Step

After you have danced the Side Step two or three times, dance steps 1 and 2 again, then turn slightly to the right on steps 3 and 4. The man will now be with his back diagonally to the centre ready to move back into the Quarter Turn to Left.

Step 1

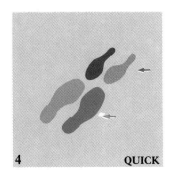 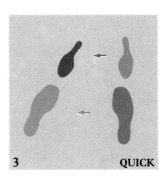 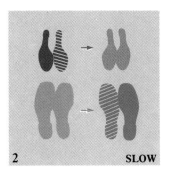 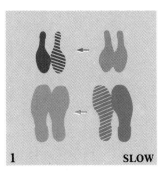

Man's steps
1 LF to the side (foot flat) and move RF halfway towards LF without weight.

2 RF to the side (foot flat) and move LF halfway towards RF without weight.

3 Turning slightly to the right, LF to the side, backing diagonally to the centre (foot flat).

4 Close RF to LF (foot flat).

Lady's steps
1 RF to the side (foot flat) and move LF halfway towards RF without weight.

2 LF to the side (foot flat) and move RF halfway towards LF without weight.

3 Turning slightly to the right, RF to the side and pointing diagonally to the centre (small step, foot flat).

4 Close LF to RF, facing diagonally to the centre (foot flat).

Side Step

First dance the Quarter Turn to Left, making less turn so that the man ends facing the wall, and the lady has her back to the wall. Now dance the Side Step two or three times. The knees should be fairly relaxed as one foot moves in towards the other on steps 1 and 2. Allow the heel of the moving foot to leave the floor. It is a good idea to count 'and' as the foot moves in, as follows: 'Slow and', 'Slow and', 'Quick', 'Quick'.

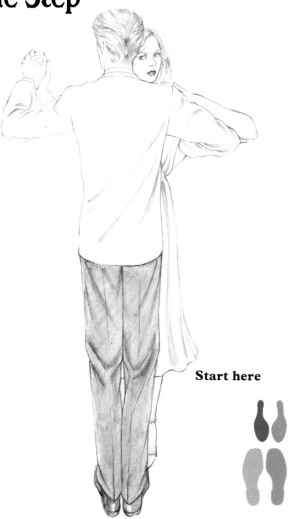

Start here

Step 4

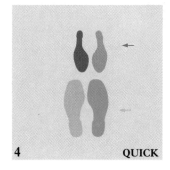

4   QUICK

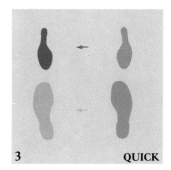

3   QUICK

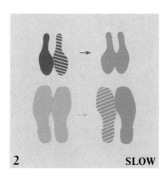

2   SLOW

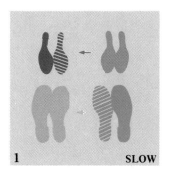

1   SLOW

4 Close RF to LF (foot flat).

3 LF to the side (foot flat).

2 RF to the side (foot flat) and move LF halfway towards RF without weight.

Man's steps
Start by facing the wall.
1 LF to the side (foot flat) and move RF halfway towards LF without weight.

4 Close LF to RF (foot flat).

3 RF to the side (foot flat).

2 LF to the side (foot flat) and move RF halfway towards LF without weight.

Lady's steps
Start with the back to the wall.
1 RF to the side (foot flat) and move LF halfway towards RF without weight.

Suggestions for joining the figures together

1 Quarter Turn to Right
  Quarter Turn to Left
  Quarter Turn to Right
  Four Natural Rock Turns
  Quarter Turn to Left.
2 Quarter Turn to Right
  Quarter Turn to Left to Promenade Position
  Three Promenade Chassés
  Man turns to Right to face lady on last two steps.
  Quarter Turn to Left.
3 Quarter Turn to Right
  Quarter Turn to Left
  Four Reverse Rock Turns.
4 Quarter Turn to Right
  Quarter Turn to Left, turning slightly less than
  usual to face wall.
  Two Side Steps
  Exit to Side Step
  Quarter Turn to Left
  At the end of the room
5 Quarter Turn to Right
  Three Natural Rock Turns. Man is now backing
  diagonally to the centre of the next line of dance.
  Quarter Turn to Left.

You can practise all these groups of figures except
Number 5 continuously, as at the end of each you will
be in your starting position again.

How to improve your Social Foxtrot

As you have noticed, the steps have not been too
difficult to learn. You have been walking forward and
back quite naturally, and these steps, coupled with
the little side and close movements, have formed the
basis of the dance. Now you can develop a more
rhythmic interpretation – a feeling of dancing rather
than walking through the steps.

Remember you can hear four beats to the bar of
music. 'One, two, three, four.' Stand with your feet
together and straighten your knees a little when you
hear beat one, bend them a little on beat two,
straighten a little on beat three and bend a little on
beat four. Try to keep these movements relaxed : the
knees should not straighten stiffly or bend sharply,
but only very, very slightly.

Now try this as you take slow walking steps
forward or back.

Step:	WALK		WALK	
Say:	1	2	3	4
Knees:	Straight	Bend	Straight	Bend

Now practise the same knee action as you take the
side and close steps.

Step:	SIDE	CLOSE	SIDE	CLOSE
Say:	1	2	3	4
Knees:	Straight	Bend	Straight	Bend

Practise as you dance your figure.

Step 1 of Quarter Turn to Right

Step 1 of Natural Rock Turn

Step 4 Quarter Turn to Left

Step 2 of Quarter Turn to Left

Starting position of Promenade Chassé : lady's side view

Step 2 of Promenade Chassé : lady's side view

Points to Remember

Do not take long steps: the dance is a social, not an exhibition dance.

Never look down. There is always a tendency to drop the eye level on the Promenade Chassé. Resist it.

Always start to dance on the first beat of the bar.

The Rock Turns are especially useful where movement is restricted on the floor and you are confined to one spot.

THE
WALTZ

The Waltz is never lacking in popularity among dancers, with its graceful turns and spins and free, flowing movement. The music is played at about 32 bars a minute, and each bar has three beats, which you can hear distinctly. The first beat is accentuated. The steps are danced in groups of three, each step to one beat of music and – unlike in the Foxtrot – all at the same speed. 'One, two, three'. In the figures described, this rhythm will never change. To begin, try the Closed Change steps. In this exercise we shall start with the right foot, but on the floor you can start with either foot. Take the weight fully on to each step. The man or lady should practise the exercise alone and start by facing the line of dance.

Step forward on your right foot, saying 'One'. Step to the side with your left foot, saying, 'Two'. Close right foot to left foot, saying 'Three'. Now step forward with your left foot, saying 'One' again. Step to the side with your right foot, saying 'Two'. Close left foot to right foot, saying 'Three'.

Repeat these steps, first starting with your right foot. Remember never to use the same foot twice in succession. Say 'Right, side, close, left, side, close', and keep saying it until you feel confident enough to try the steps to music. Listen carefully for the beats in the music and step forward on the first beat which is accentuated. Now try the steps taking each first step back instead of forward. In other words, back on right foot, side, close, back on left foot, side, close. Practise as before, then try four sets of steps forward and four back. If you have a partner, practise this together, the man moving forward while the lady moves back, and vice versa.

Natural Turn and Right Foot Closed Change

If you have practised the Closed Change steps, you should find the pattern of the Natural Turn quite easy. To dance it, the man does a forward Change step, followed by a backward Change step, while at the same time the lady does a backward Change step, followed by a forward Change step, both turning to the right throughout. Steps 1–6 are the Natural Turn, steps 7–9 are the Right Foot Closed Change.

Note that the second step of the Right Foot Closed Change is slightly forward for the man

and slightly back for the lady. This is because when you are both dancing with confidence the swing of your bodies makes these positions the natural ones for your feet.

When you have danced the following nine steps, follow them with the Reverse Turn and Left Foot Closed Change.

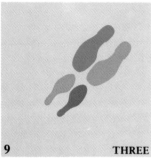

9 THREE

9 Close RF to LF (on toes).
Lower the right heel as you start the next step.

9 Close LF to RF (on toes).
Lower left heel as you start the next step.

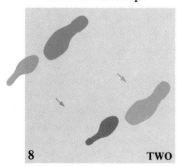

8 TWO

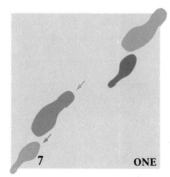

7 ONE

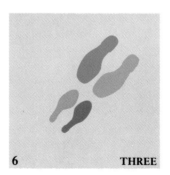

6 THREE

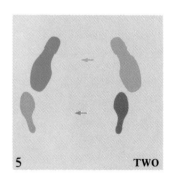

5 TWO

8 LF to the side and slightly forward (on toe).

7 Lower left heel. RF forward (heel first).

6 Close LF to RF, facing diagonally to the centre (on toes).

5 Still turning to the right, RF to the side and pointing diagonally to the centre (on toe).

8 RF to the side and slightly back (on toe).

7 Lower right heel. LF back (on toe, then lower to heel).

6 Still turning, close RF to LF, backing diagonally to the centre (on toes).

5 Still turning to the right, LF to the side, backing to diagonally the centre (on toes).

Start here

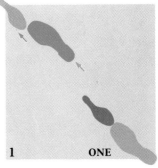

Step 7

Step 5

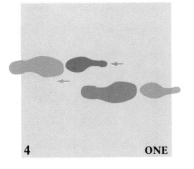

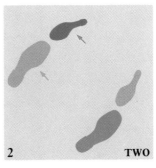

4   **ONE**

3   **THREE**

2   **TWO**

1   **ONE**

Man's steps
Start by facing diagonally to the wall.

1 RF forward, starting to turn to the right (heel first).

4 Lower right heel. LF back, starting to turn to the right (on toe, then lower to heel).

3 Still turning, close RF to LF, backing to the line of dance (on toes).

2 Still turning to the right, LF to the side, backing diagonally to the centre (on toes).

Lady's steps
Start with the back diagonal to the wall.

1 LF back, starting to turn to the right (on toe, then lower to heel).

4 Lower left heel. RF forward, starting to turn to the right (heel first).

3 Close LF to RF, facing the line of dance (on toes).

2 Still turning to the right, RF to the side and pointing to the line of dance (on toe).

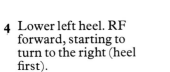

33

Reverse Turn and Left Foot Closed Change

These two figures have the same pattern as the Natural Turn and Right Foot Closed Change, except that you start with the other foot and turn left instead of right. Steps 1–6 are the Reverse Turn. Steps 7–9 are the Left Foot Closed Change. The Closed Change acts as a link between turns, and the following two figures can be danced just as well before as after the preceding two.

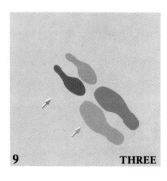

9   THREE

9 Close LF to RF (on toes).
Lower left heel as you start the next step.

9 Close RF to LF (on (toes).
Lower right heel as you start the next step.

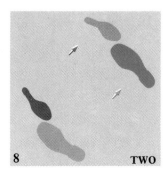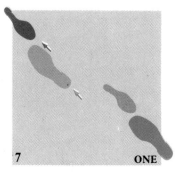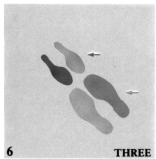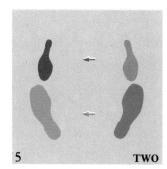

8   TWO   7   ONE   6   THREE   5   TWO

8 RF to the side and slightly forward (on toes).

7 Lower right heel. LF forward (heel first).

6 Close RF to LF, facing diagonally to the wall (on toes).

5 Still turning to the left, LF to the side and pointing diagonally to the wall (on toe).

8 LF to the side and slightly back (on toe).

7 Lower left heel. RF back (on toe, then lower to heel).

6 Still turning, close LF to RF, backing diagonally to the wall (on toes).

5 Still turning to the left, RF to the side, backing to the wall (on toes).

Start here

Starting to take step 1

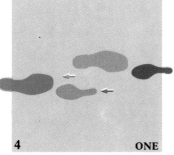

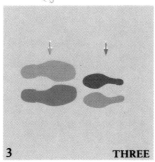

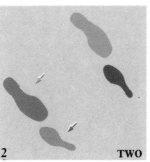

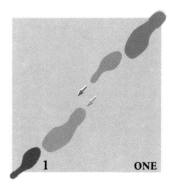

| **4** | ONE | **3** | THREE | **2** | TWO | **1** | ONE |

4 Lower left heel. RF back, starting to turn to the left (on toe, then lower to heel).

3 Still turning, close LF to RF, backing to the line of dance (on toes).

2 Still turning to the left, RF to the side, backing diagonally to the wall (on toes).

Man's steps
Start by facing diagonally to the centre.
1 LF forward, starting to turn to the left (heel first).

4 Lower right heel. LF forward, starting to turn to the left (heel first).

3 Close RF to LF, facing the line of dance (on toes).

2 Still turning to the left, LF to the side and pointing to the line of dance (on toe).

Lady's steps
Start with the back diagonal to the centre.
1 RF back, starting to turn to the left (on toe, then lower to heel).

Hesitation Change

The Hesitation Change can be used instead of the Natural Turn and Right Foot Closed Change to lead straight into a Reverse Turn. It will follow a Left Foot Closed Change.

The first three steps are the same as those of the Natural Turn.

Remember not to change weight on step 6.

Step 6

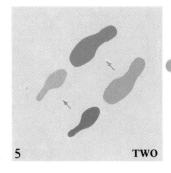

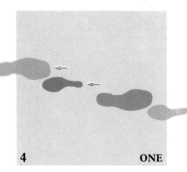

| 6 THREE | 5 TWO | 4 ONE |

6 Close LF to RF without changing weight allowing the left heel to leave the floor.

6 Close RF to LF without changing weight allowing the right heel to leave the floor.

5 Turning to the right on LF, RF to the side, both feet facing diagonally to the centre (small step, feet flat).

5 Still turning to the right, LF to the side, backing diagonally to the centre (heels just off the floor, then lower left heel).

4 Lower right heel. LF back, starting to turn to the right (on toe, then lower to heel).

4 Lower left heel. RF forward, starting to turn to the right (heel first).

36

Step 4

Start here

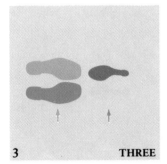

3   THREE

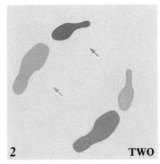

2   TWO

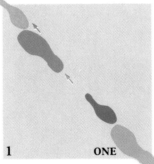

1   ONE

3 Still turning, close RF to LF backing to the line of dance (on toes).

2 Still turning to the right, LF to the side, backing diagonally to the centre (on toes).

Man's steps
Start by facing diagonally to the wall.
1 RF forward, starting to turn to the right (heel first).

3 Close LF to RF, facing the line of dance (on toes).

2 Still turning to the right, RF to the side and pointing to the line of dance (on toe).

Lady's steps
Start with the back diagonal to the wall.
1 LF back, starting to turn to the right (on toe, then lower to heel).

Outside Change

This is a very useful figure when there is no room for you to move towards the centre of the room after a complete Natural Turn.

You will first dance 1–3 of the Natural Turn, turning a little less to back diagonally to the centre.

On step 6 the man should try to keep his body facing the wall, even though his left foot will be facing diagonally to the wall. The lady should keep her back to the wall. This ensures that both partners' bodies are in the ideal position when the man steps outside on the last step – which becomes the first step of the Natural Turn.

Step 7

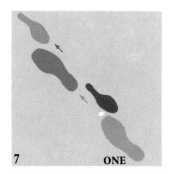
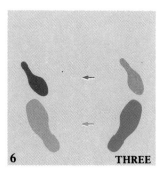
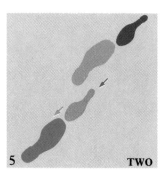
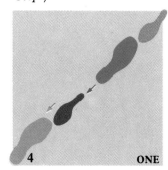

| 7 ... ONE | 6 ... THREE | 5 ... TWO | 4 ... ONE |

7 Lower left heel. RF forward, outside partner on her right side (heel first).

6 Still turning to the left, LF to the side and slightly forward, pointing diagonally to the wall (on toes).

5 RF back, starting to turn to the left (on toe).

4 Lower right heel. LF back (on toe, then lower to heel).

7 Lower right heel. LF back (on toe, then lower to heel).

6 Still turning to the left, RF to the side and slightly back, backing diagonally to the wall (on toes).

5 LF forward, starting to turn to the left (on toes).

4 Lower left heel. RF forward (heel first).

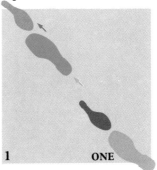

Step 2

Start here

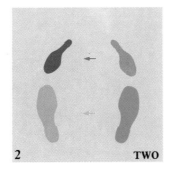

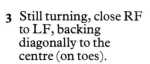

3   THREE

2   TWO

1   ONE

3 Still turning, close RF to LF, backing diagonally to the centre (on toes).

2 Still turning to the right, LF to the side and backing to the centre (on toes).

Man's steps
Start by facing diagonally to the wall.
1 RF forward, starting to turn to the right (heel first).

3 Close LF to RF, facing diagonally to the centre (on toes).

2 Still turning to the right, RF to the side and pointing diagonally to the centre (on toe).

Lady's steps
Start with the back diagonal to the wall.
1 LF back, starting to turn to the right (on toe, then lower to heel).

39

Natural Spin Turn

This is one of the most popular and characteristic figures of the Waltz. It is most useful when danced near the end of the room.

Again, the first three steps are the same as those of the Natural Turn. Step 4 is a shorter step than usual. The man should keep his left foot flat as he turns with his weight on the ball of the left foot, keeping the right foot forward throughout the step. The lady should keep her left foot back throughout the step. The lady should step between the man's feet on step 4, while the man steps between her feet on step 5. Steps 7–9 are the same as steps 4–6 of the Reverse Turn.

Follow this figure with a Left Foot Closed Change.

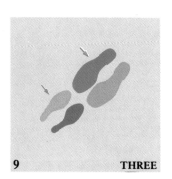

9   THREE

9 Close RF to LF, facing diagonally to the wall (on toes).
Lower right heel as you start the next step.

9 Still turning, close LF to RF, backing diagonally to the wall (on toes).
Lower left heel as you start the next step.

Step 6

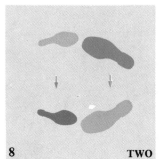

8   TWO

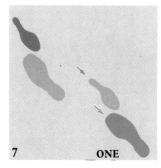

7   ONE

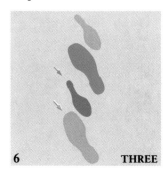

6   THREE

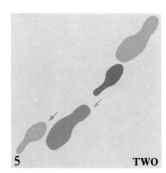

5   TWO

8 Still turning to the left, LF to the side and pointing diagonally to the wall (on toe).

7 Lower left heel. RF back, starting to turn to the left (on toe, then lower to heel).

6 Turning to the right on RF, LF to the side and slightly back, backing diagonally to the centre (on toes).

5 RF forward, facing diagonally to the wall (heel first).

8 Still turning to the left, RF to the side, backing to the wall (on toes).

7 Lower right heel. LF forward, starting to turn to the left (heel first).

6 Turning to the right on LF, brush RF to LF then RF diagonally forward, facing diagonally to the centre (on toes).

5 LF back and slightly to the left, backing diagonally to the wall (on toe).

40

Start here

Step 4

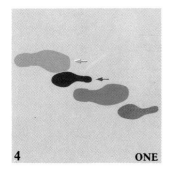

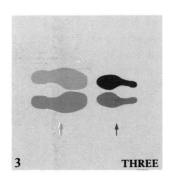

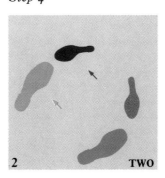

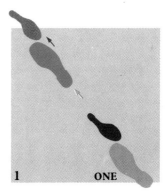

| **4** ... ONE | **3** ... THREE | **2** ... TWO | **1** ... ONE |

4 Lower right heel. LF back and turn right on LF to face diagonally to new wall. Toe, then lower to heel.

3 Still turning, close RF to LF backing to the line of dance (on toes).

2 Still turning to the right, LF to the side, backing diagonally to the centre (on toes).

Man's steps
Start near the end of the room, facing diagonally to the wall.
1 RF forward, starting to turn to the right (heel first).

4 Lower left heel. RF forward. Turn to right on RF to back diagonally to new wall (heel first, then turn on the ball of RF).

3 Close LF to RF, facing the line of dance (on toes).

2 Still turning to the right, RF to the side and pointing to the line of dance (on toe).

Lady's steps
Start near the end of the room with the back diagonal to the wall.
1 LF back, starting to turn to the right (toe, then lower to heel).

Suggestions for joining the figures together

1 Natural Turn
   RF Closed Change
   Reverse Turn
   LF Closed Change.
2 Reverse Turn
   LF Closed Change
   Natural Turn
   RF Closed Change.
3 LF Closed Change
   Steps 1–3 of Natural Turn
   Outside Change
   Natural Turn
   RF Closed Change
   Reverse Turn.
4 Hesitation Change
   Reverse Turn
   LF Closed Change.
At the end of the room
5 After a LF Closed Change
   use a Natural Turn to bring the man facing
   diagonally to the wall of the next line of dance.
   Follow this with another Natural Turn.
6 After a LF Closed Change
   dance a Natural Spin Turn and
   steps 4–6 of Reverse Turn to bring the man facing
   diagonally to the wall of the next line of dance.
   Follow with a LF Closed Change and Natural
   Turn.

Groups of figures 1 to 4 can be repeated
continuously for practice.

How to improve your Waltz

When you are learning the figures do not worry too
much about the footwork (the correct use of heels and
toes). Later, however, you will derive more pleasure
from the dance if you use your feet precisely.

Normally you are down on your heel on the first
beat of music and rising to your toes on the second and
third beats.

Practise the following exercise to help you develop
the correct use of your knees, feet and ankles.

Stand with your feet together, high on both toes.
Lower your heels to the floor and relax your knees
slightly. Say 'One'.

Lift your heels slightly off the floor. Say 'Two'.

Rise high to your toes and straighten, but do not
stiffen, your knees. Say 'Three'.

Repeat the procedure as many times as you can
without losing your balance or becoming tired. When
you lower on 'One', avoid dropping your heels to the
floor with a bang. Try to control the lowering,
keeping your weight forward over the balls of the feet.
It will help strengthen your feet and ankles if you take
your shoes off.

Step 4 of Natural Turn

Step 1 of Reverse Turn

After you have practised the exercise, try it to
music.

Then try to use the knees and feet in the way
described when you are actually dancing a Waltz on
the floor. The correct use of the knees will help you to
achieve more movement.

Step 3 of Natural Turn before dancing Outside Change

Step 1 of Outside Change

Step 1 of Natural Turn started outside partner : man's back view

Step 1 of Natural Turn started outside partner : lady's back view

Points to Remember

When the floor is small or crowded, keep your steps shorter. It is easy to adapt the Waltz to these conditions.

When you are stepping back try to keep your body towards your partner and try to lower the heel gradually, not to drop your weight back on to it.

On the last step of the Outside Change, both partners should have both their feet in a direct line. In other words, the man's right foot must be on the same line as his left foot and the lady's left foot must be on the same line as her right foot. This helps to improve the body position of both partners relative to each other.

—THE—
QUICKSTEP

The Quickstep is a bright, happy dance, and, like the Waltz, it should have free, flowing movement. Unlike the Waltz, however, it is not easy to adapt it to small, crowded spaces. Under these conditions it is better to use a speeded-up version of the Social Foxtrot. Quickstep music is played at about 50 bars a minute, and, as in the Social Foxtrot, there are four beats to the bar. If you can hear the steady 'One, two, three, four' beats of the Foxtrot you will have no trouble discerning them in the Quickstep. You will just have to move faster! As in the Social Foxtrot, a Slow step takes two beats and a Quick step one beat. Try walking to the music as you did in the Foxtrot, first doing slow steps then quick steps. Do not worry too much about the footwork until you can dance the figures with reasonable confidence. However, when you can master the correct use of your heels and toes it will help you to achieve lightness and an easier movement. The knees should be used in the same kind of way as in the Waltz. Relax them when you lower to the heel and straighten them when rising to the toes. Because of the speed of the music, the relaxation will be less than in the Waltz. You will find there is just not time to relax them so much. The step patterns have many similarities to those of the Waltz and the Social Foxtrot, so you should not have too much trouble learning the figures.

Quarter Turn to Right, Progressive Chassé and Forward Lock

Steps 1–4 are the Quarter Turn to Right, steps 5–8 are the Progressive Chassé and steps 9–13 are the Forward Lock.

The man should keep his body in a position between facing the wall and facing diagonally to the wall on steps 6 to 13, the lady matching him.

The last step will lead directly into the next figure, the Natural Turn. Or it can form the first step of a repeat of this figure, which can be practised over and over again.

Continued overleaf

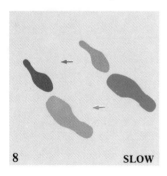

8 SLOW

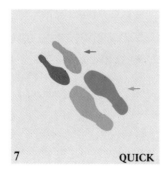

7 QUICK

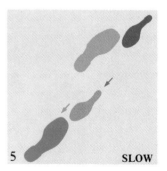

6 QUICK

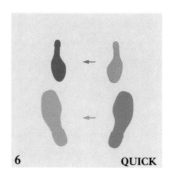

5 SLOW

8 LF to the side and slightly forward (on toes).

7 Close RF to LF, facing diagonally to the wall (on toes).

6 Still turning to the left, LF to the side and pointing diagonally to the wall (on toe).

5 Lower left heel. RF back, starting to turn to the left (on toe, then lower to heel).

8 RF to the side and slightly back (on toes).

7 Still turning, close LF to RF, backing diagonally to the wall (on toes).

6 Still turning to the left, RF to the side, backing to the wall. (Toes).

5 Lower right heel. LF forward, starting to turn to the left (heel first).

46

Start here

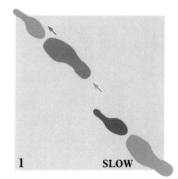

Steps 9 and 13 (overleaf)

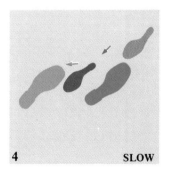

4 SLOW

3 QUICK

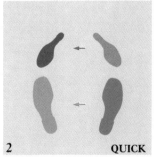

2 QUICK

1 SLOW

4 LF to the side and slightly back (on toes).

3 Still turning, close RF to LF, backing diagonally to the centre (on toes).

2 Still turning to the right, LF to the side backing to the centre (on toes).

Man's steps
Start by facing diagonally to the wall.
  1 RF forward, starting to turn to the right (heel first).

4 RF diagonally forward (on toes).

3 Close LF to RF, facing diagonally to the centre (on toes).

2 Still turning to the right, RF to the side and pointing diagonally to the centre (on toe).

Lady's steps
Start with the back diagonal to the wall.
  1 LF back, starting to turn to the right (on toe, then lower to heel).

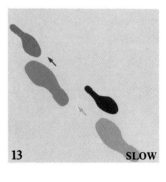

13   SLOW

13 Lower left heel. RF forward, outside partner on her right side (heel first).

Step 12   **13** Lower right heel. LF back (on toe, then lower to heel).

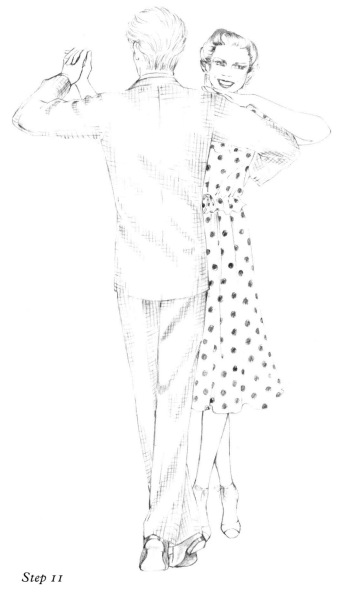

Step 11

Continued from previous page

 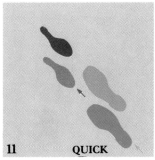 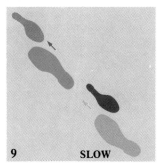

| 12 SLOW | 11 QUICK | 10 QUICK | 9 SLOW |

12 LF diagonally forward (on toes).

11 Cross RF behind LF (on toes).

10 Left foot diagonally forward (on toes).

Man's steps

9 Lower left heel. RF forward, outside partner on her right side (heel first).

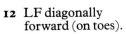

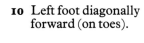

12 RF diagonally back (on toes).

11 Cross LF in front of RF (on toes).

10 RF back (on toe).

Lady's steps

9 Lower right heel. LF back (on toe, then lower to heel).

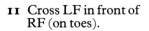

Natural Turn

This figure is danced at the end of the room. It can be danced after the Forward Lock, in which case the man's first step will be outside his partner. Follow the figure with the Quarter Turn to Right on the next line of dance.

The first four steps are the same as those of the Waltz Natural Turn. The Natural Spin Turn as described in the Waltz could be used in place of the Natural Turn. The rhythm would be 'Slow, Quick, Quick, Slow, Slow, Slow.' The man would end backing diagonally to the centre of the next line of dance and would then dance the Progressive Chassé and Forward Lock (steps 5–13 on the previous page).

Step 6

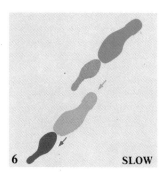 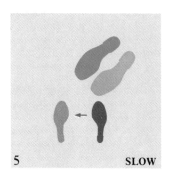 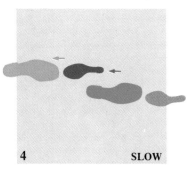

6 SLOW   **5** SLOW   **4** SLOW

6 LF forward, diagonally to the wall (heel first).

5 Turning to the right on LF, RF to the side, facing diagonally to the wall of the next line of dance (very small step, feet flat).

4 Lower right heel. LF back, starting to turn to the right (on toe, then lower to heel).

6 Still turning, RF back, diagonally to the wall (on toe, then lowering to heel).

5 Still turning to the right, LF to the side, backing to the next line of dance (heels just off the floor).

4 Lower left heel. RF forward, starting to turn to the right (heel first).

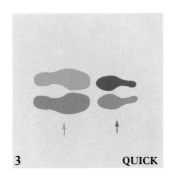 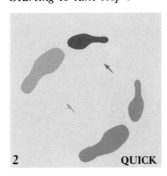 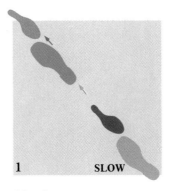

Starting to take step 6

Start here

3   QUICK

2   QUICK

1   SLOW

3 Still turning, close RF to LF, backing to the line of dance (on toes).

2 Still turning to the right, LF to the side, backing diagonally to the centre (on toes).

Man's steps
Start near the end of the room, facing diagonally to the wall.
1 RF forward, starting to turn to the right (heel first).

3 Close LF to RF, facing the line of dance (on toes).

2 Still turning to the right, RF to the side and pointing to the line of dance (on toe).

Lady's steps
Start near the end of the room, with the back diagonal to the wall.
1 LF back, starting to turn to the right (on toe, then lower to heel).

51

Natural Hesitation, Turn to Chassé and Reverse Turn with Progressive Chassé ending

The Natural Hesitation Turn is the same as the Hesitation Change in the Waltz (see page 36). The rhythm is 'Slow, Quick, Quick, Slow, Slow, Slow.' The Chassé Reverse Turn (steps 1–4 here) is the same as the first four steps of the Waltz Reverse Turn. You will then dance the Progressive Chassé (steps 5–8) which you have already learned, but the first step will back the line of dance.

Follow this figure with the Forward Lock Step.

You could also dance the Natural Hesitation Turn near the end of the room. Make less turn on steps 5 and 6 of this figure (see page 36). The man will end facing diagonally to the centre of the next line of dance to continue into the Chassé Reverse Turn.

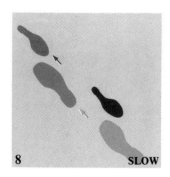 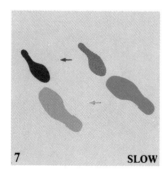 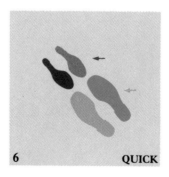 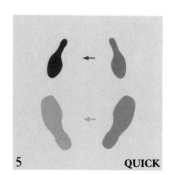

8 SLOW	7 SLOW	6 QUICK	5 QUICK
8 Lower left heel. RF forward, outside partner on her right side (heel first).	**7** LF to the side and slightly forward (on toes).	**6** Close RF to LF, facing diagonally to the wall (on toes).	**5** Still turning to the left, LF to the side and pointing diagonally to the wall (on toe).
8 Lower right heel. LF back (on toe, then lower to heel).	**7** RF to the side and slightly back (on toes).	**6** Still turning, close LF to RF, backing diagonally to the wall (on toes).	**5** Still turning to the left, RF to the side, backing to the wall (on toes).

Start here

Step 8

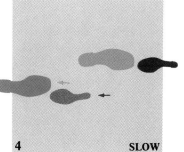

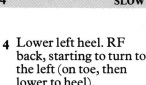

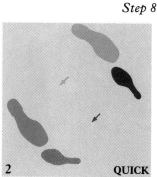

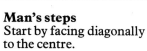

| 4 SLOW | 3 QUICK | 2 QUICK | 1 SLOW |

Man's steps
Start by facing diagonally to the centre.
1 LF forward, starting to turn to the left (heel first).

Lady's steps
Start with the back diagonal to the centre.
1 RF back, starting to turn to the left (on toe, then lower to heel).

4 Lower left heel. RF back, starting to turn to the left (on toe, then lower to heel).

3 Still turning, close LF to RF, backing to the line of dance (on toes).

2 Still turning to the left, RF to the side, backing diagonally to the wall (on toes).

4 Lower right heel. LF forward, starting to turn to the left (heel first).

3 Close RF to LF, facing the line of dance (on toes).

2 Still turning to the left, LF to the side and pointing to the line of dance (on toe).

53

Suggestions for joining the figures together

1 Quarter Turn to Right
  Progressive Chassé
  Forward Lock.
2 Quarter Turn to Right
  Progressive Chassé
  Natural Hesitation Turn
  Chassé Reverse Turn with Progressive Chassé
  ending
  Forward Lock.
3 Dance group of figures 1, approaching the end of
  the room, then dance the Natural Turn. This ends
  with the man facing diagonally to the wall of the
  next line of dance.
4 Dance group of figures 1, approaching the end of
  the room, then dance the Natural Spin Turn of the
  Waltz. This ends with the man backing diagonally
  to the centre of the next line of dance. Progressive
  Chassé.
  Forward Lock into Quarter Turn to Right or into
  Natural Hesitation Turn.

Groups of figures 1 and 2 can be repeated
continuously for practice.

Step 2 of Quarter Turn to Right

How to improve your Quickstep

At the end of the Progressive Chassé or the Forward
Lock the man must be careful not to turn his body too
much to the left before stepping outside his partner on
his right foot. He must try to keep his body in a
position between facing the wall and facing diagonally
to the wall, otherwise he will form an ugly body line
with his partner – and, in addition, he will probably
have found himself stepping forward with his left heel
instead of his left toe on the previous step. This latter
fault is common and detracts from the lightness of the
dance. It helps, when practising the Quarter Turn to
Right, Progressive Chassé and Forward Lock, to try
and rise a little higher on the toes on steps 4, 8 and 12.

Say, as you dance the first 12 steps of those figures,
'Down, toe, toe, higher, down, toe, toe, higher, down,
toe, toe, higher'.

When you have danced two Quick steps be careful
not to hurry the next step, which will always be a
Slow in the figures described. There is often a
tendency to rush this Slow step, as a result of the
momentum gained from the Quicks. If you feel that
you are doing this, try to overcome it by saying as you
dance, 'Slow, Quick, not so Quick, Slow'.

You will have noticed that there are several steps
danced outside the partner in the Quickstep. Read
again about the last step of the Outside Change in the
Waltz (see page 43) to remind you to take these steps
with your feet in a direct line with each other.

Step 2 of Forward Lock

Step 1 of Progressive Chassé

Steps 1 and 5 of Forward Lock

Step 3 of Forward Lock

Starting to close on step 6 of Natural Hesitation Turn

Points to Remember

This is a quick dance, and the man must always look where he is going. If he is heading for a collision, he must put the brakes on.

The man must not turn his head to the right when turning right – it will upset the balance of the partners and be uncomfortable for the lady.

On Step 4 of the Natural Turn the lady should remember to lower the left heel as she starts to move

the right foot forward. If the lady does not give herself time to do this she will step forward too quickly – making it difficult for her partner to lead her into the next step – and will also probably step forward on her right toe, not heel, which will result in rather a short step. This also applies to step 4 of the Natural Hesitation Turn and step 4 of the Natural Spin Turn.

THE TANGO

The Tango is as exciting to dance as it is to listen to. The music conjures up visions of Rudolph Valentino and Spanish ladies with roses between their teeth, but the Tango of today has a more modern look and, contrary to popular belief, is one of the easiest dances for the beginner to learn. There is no rise on to the toes to create balance problems, and the dance incorporates many walks, which allow the dancer plenty of time to think about what he or she is doing. As you will see in the illustrations of the hold on page 17, the man's right hand is a little further around the lady than is usual, as she is held slightly more towards his right side. To balance this, the extended joined hands (the man's left, the lady's right) are brought in fractionally from the elbow towards the head. The lady's right elbow should point towards the floor, and she must place her left hand further to the back of the man's right arm than in other dances. Study the illustration carefully. The music is played at about 33 bars a minute, and each bar contains two beats, the first accented. A slow step takes one beat, a Quick step half a beat.

The Walks are generally curved to the left. To practise, the man starts by facing diagonally to the wall and closes his feet with the right foot slightly back – right toe beside the left instep. The lady stands with her back diagonally to the wall, feet closed, with her left foot slightly forward – left heel beside the right instep. This is also the position of the closing step of most figures. Next, the man should imagine a big circle drawn on the floor and walk forward on the line of this circle, the lady walking back. The feet will be slightly angled towards the centre of the circle, and the right side of the body will be slightly in advance of the left side. As the foot starts to move keep it in contact with the floor for a few inches, then just lift it very slightly before placing it in position. Now learn the figures, and pay special attention to the section telling you how to improve your Tango.

Closed Promenade

The first two steps of this figure move along the line of dance in Promenade Position. On steps 3 and 4 the man turns the lady to face him again by exerting a little pressure on her back through his fingers – but taking care to keep his hand flat.

Lead into the Closed Promenade by dancing the Two Walks and Progressive Link. Practise repeating both figures.

Step 2

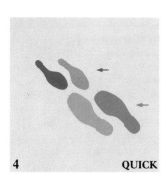

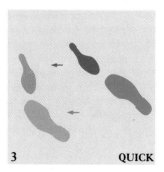

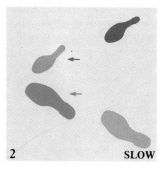

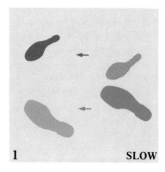

4   QUICK

3   QUICK

2   SLOW

1   SLOW

4 Close RF to LF, RF slightly back (foot flat).

4 Close LF to RF, LF slightly forward (foot flat).

3 LF to the side and slightly forward, turning the lady to face you (inside edge of ball of foot first, then flat).

3 Turning to the left to face partner, RF to the side and slightly back, backing diagonally to wall (inside edge of ball of foot first, then flat).

2 RF forward and across the LF in Promenade Position (heel first).

2 LF forward and across the RF in Promenade Position (heel first).

Man's steps
Start by facing diagonally to the wall in Promenade Position.
1 LF to the side in Promenade Position (heel first).

Lady's steps
Start by facing diagonally to the centre in Promenade Position.
1 RF to side in Promenade Position (heel first).

Two Walks and Progressive Link

Steps 1 and 2 are the Two Walks, steps 3 and 4 the Progressive Link. The Progressive Link is used to reach the Promenade Position, in which the man's right side and the lady's left side are in contact, and the two bodies form a V shape (study the illustration on page 16). The man turns the lady to this position by turning his body slightly to the right on the last step, and at the same time exerting a little pressure on her back through the heel of his right hand. On step 4 the lady will turn to Promenade Position on the ball of her right foot, not lowering the heel until she has completed her turn. She will then quickly place her left foot to the side and slightly back on the inside edge of the ball of the foot, then lowering the left heel and raising the right heel so that she is on the inside edge of the ball of the right foot.

Start here

Steps 1 and 3

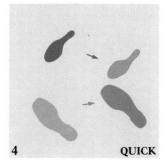

4   QUICK

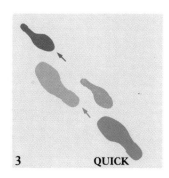

3   QUICK

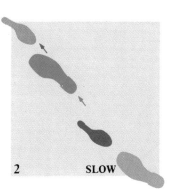

2   SLOW

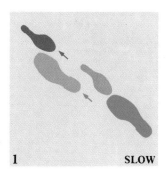

1   SLOW

4 RF to the side and slightly back. (Inside edge of RF first, then flat. Raise left heel slightly off floor. Inside edge of ball of LF).

4 Turn to right on RF to face diagonally to centre. LF to side and slightly back in Promenade Position. (Notes on footwork above).

3 LF forward (heel first).

3 RF back (on ball of foot).

2 RF forward (heel first).

2 LF back (on ball of foot, then lower to heel).

Man's steps
Start by facing diagonally to the wall.
1 LF forward (heel first).

Lady's steps
Start with the back diagonally to the wall.
1 RF back (on ball of foot, then lower to heel).

Walk into Rock Turn

The Walk into Rock Turn can be used after the Two Walks, Progressive Link and Closed Promenade, and this combination of figures should be practised repeatedly.

Step 6

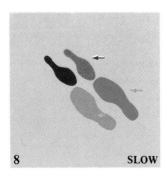 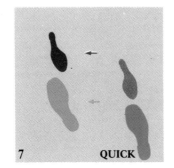 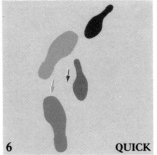 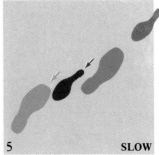

| 8   SLOW | 7   QUICK | 6   QUICK | 5   SLOW |

8 Close RF to LF, slightly back (foot flat).

7 Still turning to the left, LF to the side and slightly forward, pointing diagonally to wall (inside edge of foot first, then flat).

6 RF back, to the centre, starting to turn to the left (on ball of foot, then lower to heel).

5 LF back about two inches (on ball of foot, then lower to heel).

8 Close LF to RF, slightly forward (foot flat).

7 Still turning to the left, RF to the side and slightly back, backing diagonally to the wall (inside edge of ball of foot first, then flat).

6 LF forward, to the centre, starting to turn to the left (heel first).

5 RF forward about two inches (heel first).

Start here

Step 3

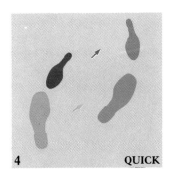 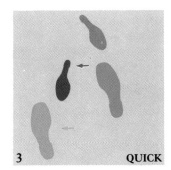 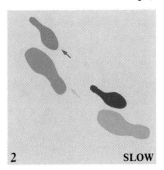 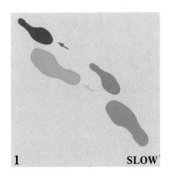

| **4** QUICK | **3** QUICK | **2** SLOW | **1** SLOW |

4 Turn RF very slightly to the right and replace weight on to it (heel first).

4 Still turning very slightly, move LF slightly to the left and place weight on to it (on ball of foot, then lower to heel).

3 Still turning to the right, LF to the side and slightly back, backing to the centre (inside edge of ball of foot first, then flat).

3 Still turning to the right, move RF slightly to the right between partner's feet and place weight on to it, facing the centre (heel first).

2 RF forward, starting to turn to the right (heel first).

2 LF back, starting to turn to the right (on ball of foot, then lower to heel).

Man's steps
Start by facing diagonally to the wall.
1 LF forward (heel first).

Lady's steps
Start with the back diagonally to the wall.
1 RF back (on ball of foot, then lower to heel).

Open Reverse Turn

Dance into the Open Reverse Turn by first dancing two Walks. The man starts the Walks with his left foot, facing diagonally to the wall, and curves them to the left until he is facing diagonally to the centre.

Follow the Open Reverse Turn with the Walk into Rock Turn.

Step 3

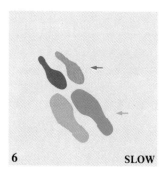

6   SLOW

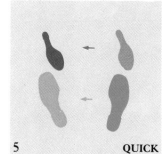

5   QUICK

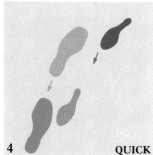

4   QUICK

6 Close RF to LF slightly back (foot flat).

6 Close LF to RF slightly forward (foot flat).

5 Still turning to the left, LF to the side and slightly forward, pointing diagonally to the wall (inside edge of foot first, then flat).

5 Still turning to the left, RF to the side and slightly back, backing diagonally to the wall (inside edge of ball of foot first, then flat).

4 Still turning to the left, RF back, backing diagonally to the centre (on ball of foot, then lower to heel).

4 Still turning to the left, LF forward, diagonally to the centre (heel first).

62

Step 1

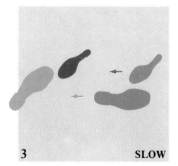

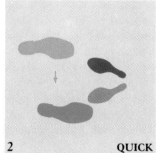

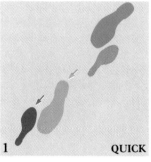

3   SLOW

2   QUICK

1   QUICK

Start here

3 Turning body very slightly to the left, LF back down the line of dance (on ball of foot, then lower to heel).

3 Turning body very slightly to the left, RF forward down the line of dance (heel first).

2 Still turning to the left, RF to the side and slightly back, backing to the line of dance (on ball of foot, then lower to heel).

2 Still turning to the left, close left heel to right heel, LF pointing to the line of dance (foot flat).

Man's steps
Start by facing diagonally to the centre.
1 LF forward, starting to turn to the left (heel first).

Lady's steps
Start with the back diagonal to the centre.
1 RF back, starting to turn to the left (on ball of foot, then lower to heel).

63

Four Step

This little figure, as its name implies, consists of four steps – all Quicks. Dance it following the Open Reverse Turn.

On step 4 the man must turn the lady to Promenade Position quite sharply, exerting pressure on her back with the heel of his hand.

Follow this figure with the Closed Promenade.

Start here

Step 1

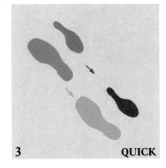

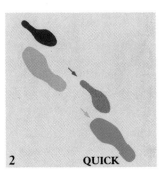

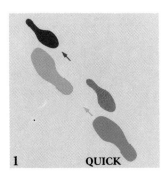

| 4 QUICK | 3 QUICK | 2 QUICK | 1 QUICK |

4 Close RF to LF, slightly back, turning lady to Promenade Position (on ball of foot, then lower to heel).

3 LF back, leading the lady to step outside on the man's right side (on ball of foot, then lower to heel).

2 RF to the side and slightly back (on ball of foot, then lower to heel).

Man's steps
Start facing diagonally to the wall.
1 LF forward (heel first).

4 Turn right on RF. Close LF to RF, slightly back in Promenade Position, facing diagonally centre (ball of foot, then on to heel).

3 RF forward, outside partner on his right side (heel first).

2 LF to the side and slightly forward (foot flat).

Lady's steps
Start with the back diagonally to the wall.
1 RF back (on ball of foot, then lower to heel).

64

Natural Promenade Turn

Dance this turn near the end of the room, after the Two Walks and Progressive Link. Follow it with a Closed Promenade along the next line of dance.

An alternative ending would be to omit step 5, and instead of turning the lady to Promenade Position make step 4 the first step of the Rock Turn. The count 'and' on step 5 indicates that the foot is placed very quickly into position and is the final part of the 'slow' on step 4.

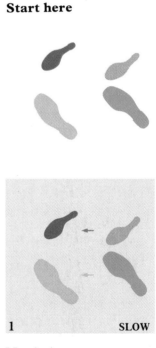

Start here

5   **and**

Man's steps

5 Place LF near to RF without weight, turning lady to Promenade Position (inside edge of ball of LF).

Lady's steps

5 Turn right on LF, to face diagonally to centre, then lower heel and place RF near to LF without weight in Promenade Position (inside edge of ball of RF).

Step 5

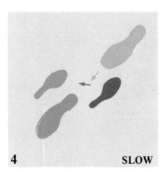

4   SLOW

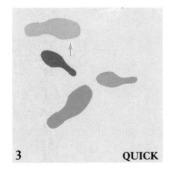

3   QUICK

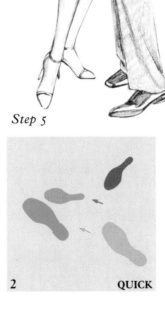

2   QUICK

1   SLOW

4 Turn to right on LF, keeping foot flat, then RF forward between lady's feet, facing diagonally to next wall (heel first).

4 Still turning to the right, LF to side and slightly back, backing diagonally to the wall of the next line of dance (on ball of foot).

3 Still turning to the right, LF to the side and slightly back, backing to the line of dance (on ball of foot, then lower to heel).

3 RF forward between partner's feet, facing the line of dance (heel first).

2 RF forward in Promenade Position, starting to turn to the right (heel first).

2 LF forward and across in Promenade Position, starting to turn to the right. LF pointing to the line of dance (heel first).

Man's steps

Start near the end of the room, facing diagonally to the wall in Promenade Position.

1 LF to side in Promenade Position (heel first).

Lady's steps

Start near the end of the room, facing diagonally to the centre in Promenade Position.

1 RF to side in Promenade Position (heel first).

Suggestions for joining the figures together

1 Two Walks: LF, RF
   Progressive Link
   Closed Promenade
   Walk into Rock Turn.

2 Two Walks, curving left to end with man facing
   diagonally to the centre: LF, RF
   Open Reverse Turn
   Four Step
   Closed Promenade
   Each of these two groups of figures can be
   repeated continuously.
   Near the end of the room

3 Two Walks: LF, RF
   Progressive Link
   Natural Promenade Turn
   Closed Promenade along the next line of dance.

4 Two Walks: LF, RF
   Open Reverse Turn
   Four Step
   Natural Promenade Turn (Omit Step 5)
   Rock Turn started diagonally to wall of the next
   line of dance.

How to improve your Tango

Although the Tango is easy to learn, a lot of practice is
required to give it expressiveness and excitement.

The knees should be very slightly flexed
throughout but this should not be exaggerated. Try to
make your legs feel strong: imagine that you have a
powerful rubber band holding your knees together
and that you have to stretch this band to its fullest
extent in order to make each step.

Slightly delay moving the foot that is not
supporting your weight, so that eventually you have to
place it in position quickly and crisply.

Take every accented quick beat – for example, the
first step of the Open Reverse Turn and the first and
third steps of the Four Step – sharply and swiftly.

When the man closes the right foot to the left on the
last step of the Closed Promenade, Rock Turn and
Open Reverse Turn, he must try to tuck his right
knee in slightly behind his left knee. This will bring
his body into the correct starting position for the
walks. The lady must also try to achieve this position
as she closes her left foot to her right.

Man's Right Foot Walk preceding the Open Reverse Turn

Step 2 of Progressive Link: lady's side view

Points to Remember

Always close your feet firmly and with deliberation.

The lady may keep her head still when she turns to
Promenade Position, but it looks more attractive if she
turns her head quite sharply to the right to look along
the line of dance. She must return her head to its
normal position as she turns to face the man.

Both partners must be careful not to look down
when in Promenade Position. The man must also keep

Step 1 of Progressive Link

Step 2 of Progressive Link

Step 3 of Closed Promenade : lady's back view

Step 4 of Closed Promenade : lady's back view

his arms still, with the elbows level, when he turns the lady to Promenade Position. He must try not to drop the right elbow or push the lady's right arm back with his left arm.

The turn to Promenade Position should always be smart and slick.

Although the instructions for backward steps state, for simplicity, 'on ball of foot, then lower to heel',

there is a distinct feeling of the inside edge of the ball of the foot touching the floor first when moving back with the left foot.

LATIN AMERICAN DANCING

Latin American dancing has greatly increased in popularity over recent years, possibly because dance floors have tended to become smaller, lending themselves to small steps and subtle, rhythmic body motion. The music, too, offers an invitation to dance that is difficult to refuse. Each dance has a different action, which it is important to study carefully when reading the introduction to the dance. If you learn the step patterns and nothing else, you will miss the pleasure of interpreting the rhythm expressively.

As with Ballroom Dancing, first learn the steps on your own. Sometimes the lady's steps are not exactly opposed to the man's as they are in Ballroom Dancing, so it it is important for the lady to dance the figures alone with good balance and control. However, the man is still the boss and it is he who decides on the figure the partners will dance. The lady should usually follow the direction of the man's body as he takes his step, although at other times the man will indicate through his arms and hands where he wants the lady to go.

When exactly opposed steps are danced with a normal hold, the partners must keep their arms still – but not stiff. The shoulders should be relaxed. Always listen carefully to the music while standing in your starting position with the weight on the correct foot. Do not rush into the dance on the wrong beat. The lady should normally wait for the man, but in the early stages of learning it will do no harm for her to give him a little help if necessary.

Normal hold for Cha Cha Cha, Samba, Rumba and Paso Doble

Normal hold for Jive. There are many different holds used in the Latin American dances: these are clearly illustrated in the figures concerned.

—THE—
CHA CHA CHA

This is the Latin American dance that most people want to learn first. The music is played at about 32–34 bars a minute, and each bar has four beats. To each four beats we dance five steps, the first two steps taking one beat each, then the following three steps (or Chassé) taking half a beat, half a beat and one beat. Each figure starts on the second beat of music. The last step of the Cha Cha Cha Chassé occurs on the first beat. Now learn the Cha Cha Cha Chassé to the left. Stand with your feet together, your weight on the right foot.

	Say
Take a small step to the side with the left foot.	Cha
Close the right foot halfway towards the left.	Cha
Left foot to the side, small step.	Cha

Now reverse the procedure and dance a Chassé to the right: right foot, left, right. Next learn the following exercise.

	Say
Step on the spot with the left foot.	Step
Step on the spot with the right foot.	Step
Cha Cha Cha Chassé to the left.	Cha Cha Cha
Step on the spot with the right foot.	Step
Step on the spot with the left foot.	Step
Cha Cha Cha Chassé to the right.	Cha Cha Cha

Practise this exercise until you can manage it with ease. Although the figures that follow are designed to start with the 'Step, Step' you will find it easier to start the dance with a Cha Cha Cha Chassé (the man to the right, the lady to the left). This is because the three beats of the Chassé are usually very easy to pick out, and tell you exactly when to do the 'Cha Cha Cha' Chassé steps. The dance does not progress around the floor, so you can choose any vacant spot on the floor from which to start. For this reason no alignments to the wall or centre etc. are given in the descriptions of the figures.

Each step is started on the ball of the foot, with the knee of that leg flexed. As the weight is taken on to the whole foot, the heel is lowered to the floor and the knee straightened. The other knee is slightly flexed, with the heel just off the floor. Allow the hips to swing naturally to the side of the stepping foot. You use this footwork on every step. That is why there are no descriptions of footwork in the figures. The knee and hip action described will not be so pronounced on the first two steps of the Chassé because there is less time to perform them. The hold is described on page 69.

Basic Movement

It is better, at the beginning, to practise this figure without turning. Say, 'Step, Replace, Cha Cha Cha', and take each Chassé directly to the side. As you become more proficient, try the turn as illustrated, gradually making a quarter turn to the left over the ten steps. When a turn is made the LF Chassé will be danced to the side and slightly back as this feels more natural.

Repeat the Basic Movement as many times as you like for practice.

Step 2

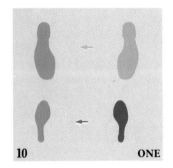

10 RF.

10 LF.

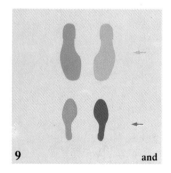

9 LF.

9 RF.

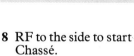

8 RF to the side to start Chassé.

8 LF to the side to start the Chassé.

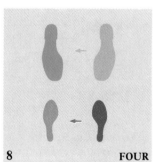

7 Replace weight forward to LF.

7 Replace weight back to RF.

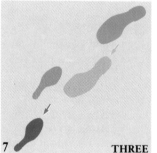

6 RF back.

6 LF forward.

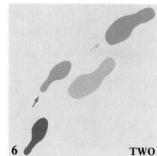

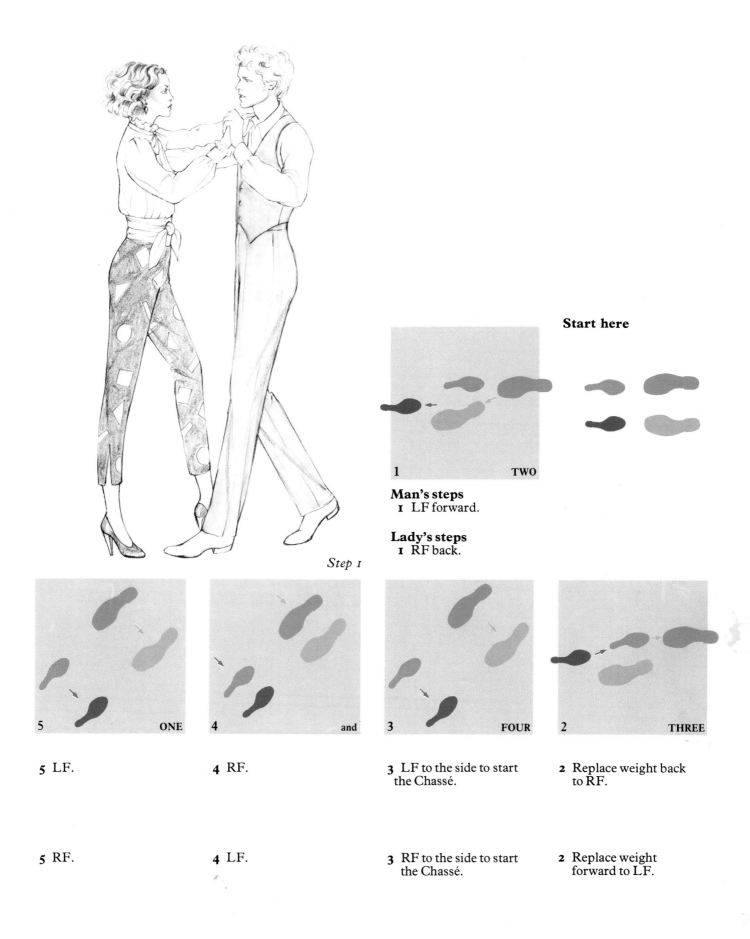

Step 1

Start here

1   **TWO**

Man's steps
1 LF forward.

Lady's steps
1 RF back.

5   **ONE**   **4**   **and**   **3**   **FOUR**   **2**   **THREE**

5 LF.

4 RF.

3 LF to the side to start the Chassé.

2 Replace weight back to RF.

5 RF.

4 LF.

3 RF to the side to start the Chassé.

2 Replace weight forward to LF.

73

Time Steps

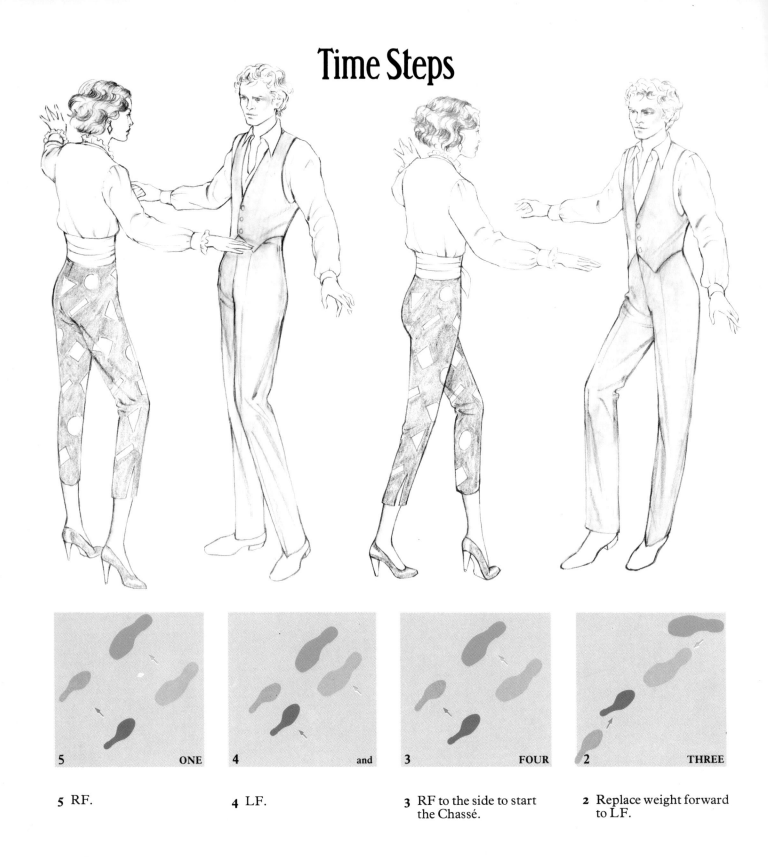

| 5 | ONE | 4 | and | 3 | FOUR | 2 | THREE |

5 RF.

4 LF.

3 RF to the side to start the Chassé.

2 Replace weight forward to LF.

5 LF.

4 RF.

3 LF to the side to start the Chassé.

2 Replace weight forward to RF.

First dance the Basic Movement and then release your partner. The partners should start each time step by facing each other, a little apart. Because there is no hold, the lady will follow the steps visually.

Dance a Left Foot Time Step and a Right Foot Time Step, then repeat these two Time Steps, making four in all.

Continue with the Basic Movement, taking up the normal hold again.

Start here

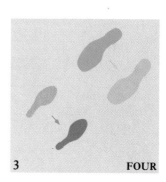

2 Replace weight forward to RF.

Man's steps — Left Foot Time Step
1 LF behind RF, with toe slightly turned out.

Far left: Step 5 of Man's Right Foot Time Step

2 Replace weight forward to LF.

Left: Step 1 of Man's Left Foot Time Step

Lady's steps—Right Foot Time Step
1 RF behind LF, with toe slightly turned out.

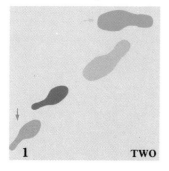

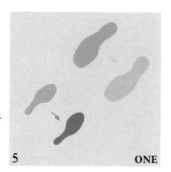

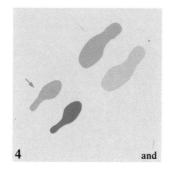

Man's steps — Right Foot Time Step
1 RF behind LF, with toe slightly turned out.

5 LF.

4 RF.

3 LF to the side to start the Chassé.

Lady's steps — Left Foot Time Step
1 LF behind RF, with toe slightly turned out.

5 RF.

4 LF.

3 RF to the side to start the Chassé

75

Lady's Turn to Right under the Arms

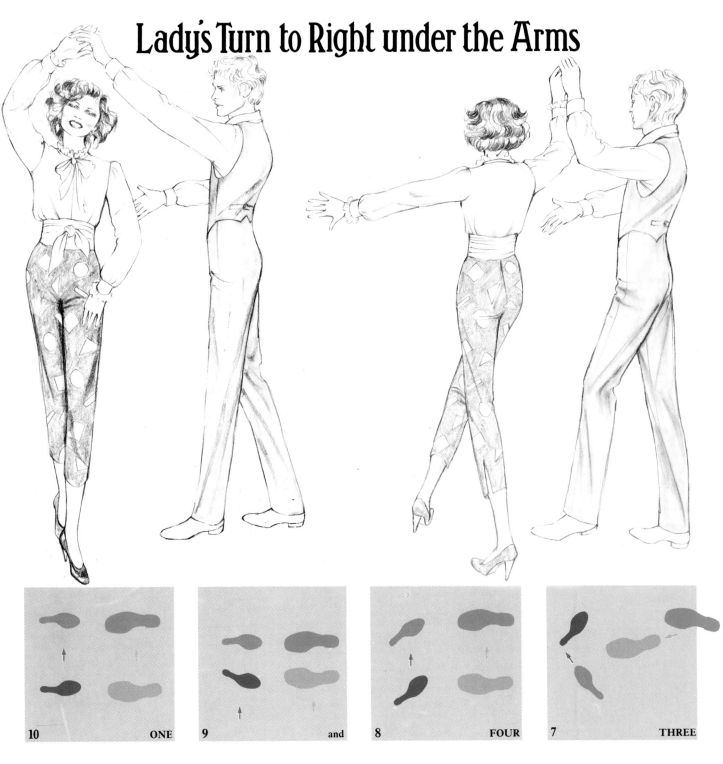

10 ONE	9 and	8 FOUR	7 THREE

10 RF, while lady still turns to right under raised arms. Take normal hold when facing partner again.

10 LF. Take normal hold when facing partner again.

9 LF.

9 RF.

8 RF to the side to start the Chassé.

8 Continuing to turn to the right under the raised arms, LF to the side to start the Chassé.

7 Replace weight forward to LF, still turning lady to her right under the joined raised arms.

7 Still turning to the right, RF forward.

Move into this figure by dancing the Basic Movement. The man then dances another Basic Movement but halfway through he turns the lady to her right under their raised arms. At the end of step 5 he must raise his left hand, which is holding the lady's right hand, to indicate to the lady that she must turn. Then, with his right hand on her back, he helps her to start her turn before releasing his hold with his right hand.

Follow this figure with the Basic Movement.

Start here

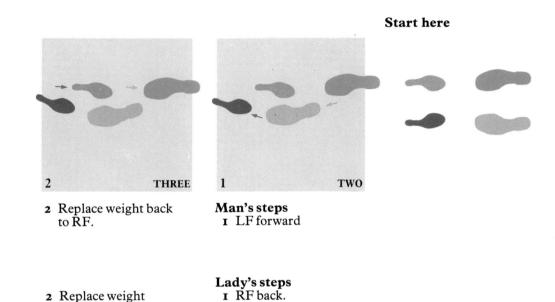

| 2 | THREE | 1 | TWO |

2 Replace weight back to RF.

Man's steps
1 LF forward

2 Replace weight forward to LF.

Lady's steps
1 RF back.

Far left: *Step 7*
Left: *Step 6*

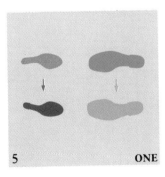 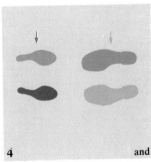

| 6 | TWO | 5 | ONE | 4 | and | 3 | FOUR |

6 RF back, while raising the left arm and starting to turn the lady to her right. Release hold with right hand.

5 LF.

4 RF.

3 LF to the side to start the Chassé.

6 Turning to the right under the joined raised arms, LF forward (man has released his hold with his right hand).

5 RF.

4 LF.

3 RF to the side to start the Chassé.

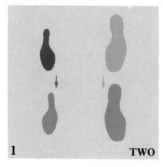

Spot Turns

These turns can be used in many different ways, as you will see later.

Here is an easy group of figures to join together. After the Basic Movement, the partners release their hold. The man now dances a Spot Turn turning to his right, while the lady

MAN TURNING TO LEFT, LADY TURNING TO RIGHT

Start here

1   **TWO**

Man's steps
Start by facing partner, a little apart, without hold.
1 Turning a quarter to the left, RF forward.

Lady's steps
Start by facing partner, a little apart, without hold.
1 Turning a quarter to the right, LF forward.

Step 2 of Man's Spot Turn to Right

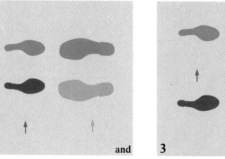

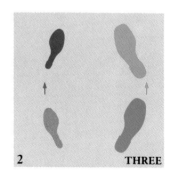

5 **ONE**	**4** **and**	**3** **FOUR**	**2** **THREE**

5 RF.

4 LF.

3 RF to the side to start the Chassé, turning a further quarter to the left to face partner again.

2 Turn a half to the left on RF, keeping LF in place, and transfer weight forward to LF.

5 LF.

4 RF.

3 LF to the side to start the Chassé, turning a further quarter to the right to face partner again.

2 Turn a half to the right on LF, keeping RF in place, and transfer weight forward to RF.

78

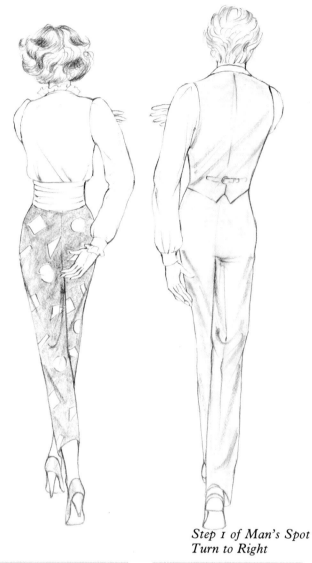

dances steps 1–5 of the Basic Movement. Then the man dances steps 6–10 of the Basic Movement, while the lady does a Spot Turn turning to her right.

The partners then resume the normal hold and continue with a Basic Movement.

MAN TURNING TO RIGHT, LADY TURNING TO LEFT

Start here

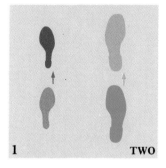
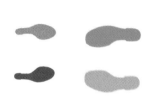

1   TWO

Man's steps
Start by facing partner, a little apart, without hold.
1 Turning a quarter to the right, LF forward.

Lady's steps
Start by facing partner, a little apart, without hold.
1 Turning a quarter to the left, RF forward.

Step 1 of Man's Spot Turn to Right

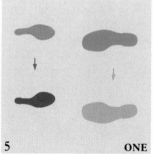

5   ONE

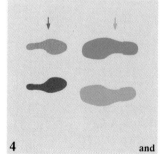

4   and

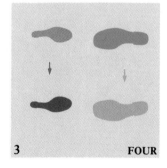

3   FOUR

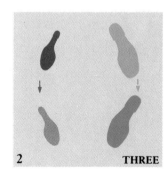

2   THREE

5 LF.

4 RF.

3 LF to the side to start the Chassé, turning a further quarter to the right to face partner again.

2 Turn a half to the right on LF, keeping RF in place, and transfer weight forward to RF.

5 RF.

4 LF.

3 RF to the side to start the Chassé, turning a further quarter to the left to face partner again.

2 Turn a half to the left on RF, keeping LF in place, and transfer weight forward to LF.

New York

Step 6

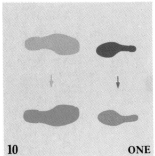

10   ONE

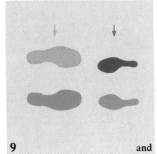

9   and

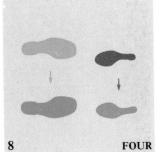

8   FOUR

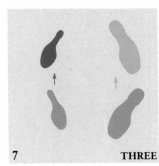

7   THREE

10 RF. Now take lady's right hand in your left hand and repeat the New York or take normal hold again.

9 LF.

8 RF to the side to start the Chassé, turning a quarter to the right to face partner again.

7 Replace weight back to LF.

10 LF. Man will take lady's right hand in his left hand to repeat the New York or will take normal hold again.

9 RF.

8 LF to the side to start the Chassé, turning a quarter to the left to face partner again.

7 Replace weight back to RF.

Move into this figure by dancing the Basic Movement. The man then releases hold with his right hand. Dance the New York, then repeat it, as explained in the text. Resume the normal hold and continue with the Basic Movement.

The man turns the lady left on the first step of the New York by taking his left hand forward. He turns her to face him again on the Chassé by returning his left arm to its original position. On step 6 he turns the lady right with his right hand. On the Chassé he turns her back with his right hand to face him again.

Start here

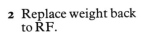

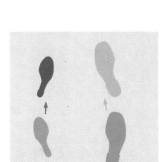

2 THREE	1 TWO

2 Replace weight back to RF.

Man's steps
1 Releasing hold with right hand and turning a quarter to the right, LF forward, turning lady to her left.

Lady's steps
1 Turning a quarter to the left, RF forward (man has released hold of lady's left hand.

2 Replace weight back to LF.

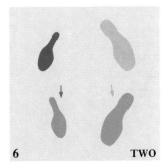

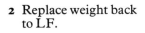

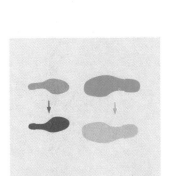

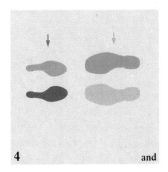

6 TWO	5 ONE	4 and	3 FOUR

6 Releasing hold with left hand and turning a quarter to the left, RF forward, turning lady to her right.

6 Turning a quarter to the right, LF forward (man has released hold of lady's right hand).

5 LF. Now take lady's left hand in your right hand.

5 RF. Man will take lady's left hand in his right hand.

4 RF.

4 LF.

3 LF to the side to start the Chassé, turning a quarter to the left to face partner again.

3 RF to the side to start the Chassé, turning a quarter to the right to face partner again.

Suggestions for joining the figures together

1 Basic Movement
  Basic Movement with Lady's Turn to Right under the Arms
  Release hold and follow with:
2 Time Steps (man start with LF, lady with RF)
  Man does Spot Turn to Right, while lady does Time Step, starting with RF
  Man does Time Step, starting with RF while lady does Spot Turn to Right
  Take normal hold.
2 Basic Movement
  New York: steps 1–10, then repeat steps 1–5. Man does not regain hold with left hand.
  Spot Turn (man turns to left, lady turns to right)
  Take normal hold.
3 Basic Movement
  Basic Movement with Lady's Turn to Right under the Arms (man does not regain hold with right hand)
  New York.
4 Dance group of figures 2 as above, but instead of resuming normal hold at end dance four Time Steps (man starts with LF, lady with RF).
  Take normal hold.

How to improve your Cha Cha Cha

You will derive more pleasure from the Cha Cha Cha if you can develop a rhythmic action. This is impossible if you take large steps. Keep the steps small, and remember to keep the ball of your foot in contact with the floor at all times. It should *never* leave the floor.

Always try to take your full weight on to the second step of each Chassé. If you do not, you will fall on to the third step and it will become too hurried: remember, the third step has a whole beat to itself. It is sometimes helpful to say to yourself 'Cha Cha Step' instead of 'Cha Cha Cha'.

When you dance a Spot Turn, make sure you are looking at your partner before you start to turn; then look at your partner as quickly as possible again as you dance the Chassé. This should help you to keep your balance, and it also adds expression to the step.

Points to Remember

When you are not holding, do not drop your arms down loosely by your sides. Extend them to the sides, below the shoulder level and sloping downwards so that the hands are at about waist level but do not hold them stiffly. Study the illustrations carefully.

Never look down, even though you may be tempted to do so because you are standing away from your partner.

When the man turns the lady under their arms, they should make sure their arms are raised high.

Correct hold for Cha Cha Cha

Step 1 of Time Step: man starting with left foot, lady with right

Starting to dance step 6 of Lady's Turn to Right under the Arms

Step 1 of Basic Movement

Step 5 of Time Step: man starting with right foot, lady with left

Step 2 of New York

THE JIVE

The Jive is a 'must' in the dancer's repertoire. It can be danced to so many pop tunes of the day, and it takes up very little room as the steps are small. The man stays on one spot while he leads the lady into underarm turns and spins. Jive music is usually played at about 40–46 bars a minute – although it can be much faster. It is wise to practise slow Jives at first. There are four beats to the bar. All the figures described have eight steps, consisting of a step back (one beat), a replacement of the weight forward (one beat) and two little three-step Chassés, each of which takes three-quarters of a beat on the first step, a quarter of a beat on the second step, and a whole beat on the third step. Each figure has a total of six beats.

To practise the Chassé, try the steps of the Cha Cha Cha Chassé, but instead of saying 'Cha Cha Cha' as you do so, say 'One a Two' with the 'a' short and crisp (this is the quarter beat). Keep the steps a little smaller in Jive than you did in the Cha Cha Cha. The Chassé can be danced in all directions: side, forward, back or turning to the right or left. Before attempting the figures, try the six steps that follow. If you have a partner, face him or her and hold both hands, using the Latin American hold illustrated on page 69 or try the steps alone.

	Say
Step back (man on left foot, lady on right).	One
Replace weight forward to front foot.	Two
Step to side and Chassé (man: left foot, right, left; lady: right foot, left, right).	Three a Four
Step to side and Chassé (man: right foot, left, right; lady: left foot, right, left).	Five a Six

Dance every step on the ball of the foot and then lower to the heel. Keep the knees relaxed but a little springy. You could also say to yourself as you are practising, 'Rock back, Rock forward, Chassé to side, Chassé to side'. Repeat the exercise until you can do it easily to the music. You should find the figures that follow quite easy. Just remember that you will dance 'Back, Replace, Chassé, Chassé' on EVERY figure. The man starts every figure with his left foot, the lady with her right.

Fallaway Rock

Fallaway Position is the same as Promenade Position – except that the couple move back instead of forward. The man turns the lady out to the Fallaway Position through a slight push with his left hand and a little pressure on her back with the heel of his right hand. He turns her to face him again through slight pressure with the fingers of the right hand as he dances the Chassé (steps 3–5).

Practise the Fallaway Rock several times in succession.

Position for steps 3–5

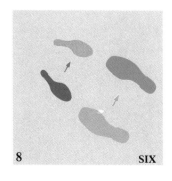 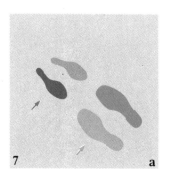 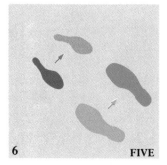 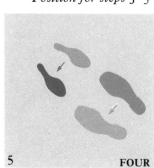

8 SIX	7 a	6 FIVE	5 FOUR

8 RF.	**7** LF.	**6** RF to the side to start the Chassé.	**5** LF, turning lady to face you.
8 LF.	**7** RF.	**6** LF to the side to start the Chassé.	**5** RF, turning to face partner.

Step *1*

Start here

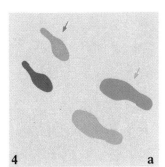
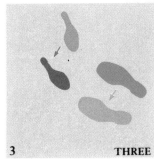
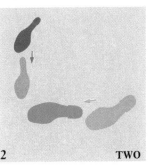
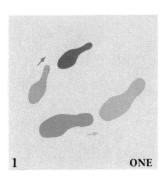

| **4** | **a** | **3** | **THREE** | **2** | **TWO** | **1** | **ONE** |

4 RF, still turning lady to her left.

3 LF to the side to start the Chassé, turning slightly to the right and starting to turn lady to her left.

2 Replace weight forward to RF.

Man's steps
1 Turning slightly to the left, LF back in Fallaway Position, turning lady to her right.

4 LF, still turning to left.

3 RF to the side to start the Chassé, starting to turn to the left.

2 Replace weight forward to LF.

Lady's steps
1 Turning to the right, RF back in Fallaway Position.

87

Change of Places from Right to Left

Lead into the figure with the Fallaway Rock. The man must always remember to raise his left arm at the end of step 5 so that the lady knows she has to go under the arch created by the raised arms. After that he must help her turn with his right hand, immediately releasing the hold when she is on her way.

When the lady is turning right under the raised arms on the second Chassé, she should not worry about the exact position of her feet – they will vary according to the speed of the turn. This figure can also be danced with a change of hands. Instead of turning the body underneath the joined hands the man must release hold completely at the end of step 5. The lady will make a solo turn and the man will catch her right hand in his right hand at the end of her turn. This is called the Handshake hold.

Step 6

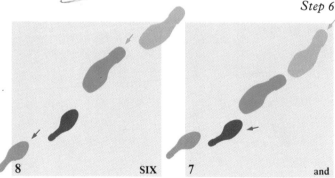
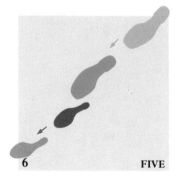
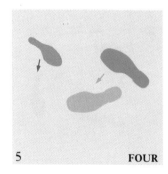

8 SIX	7 and	6 FIVE	5 FOUR

8 RF. Lower the arms at the end of the lady's turn. You are now in Open Facing Position.

7 LF, still turning lady to her right.

6 Turning to the left, RF forward to start the Chassé. Release hold with the right hand and turn the lady to her right under the raised joined hands.

5 LF, raising left arm and starting to turn lady to her right.

8 LF back, still turning right. You are now in Open Facing Position. The man will have lowered the joined hands.

7 RF, still turning to right.

6 Start the Chassé with LF turning to right under the raised arms.

5 RF, turning slightly to right.

Start here

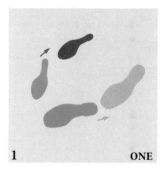

Step 5

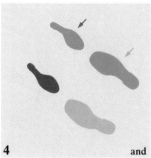 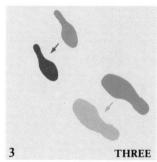 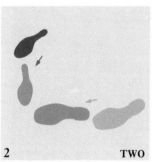 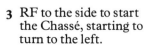

| **4** and | **3** THREE | **2** TWO | **1** ONE |

Man's steps

4 RF, still turning lady to her left to face you.

3 LF to the side to start the Chassé, starting to turn the lady to her left.

2 Replace weight forward to RF.

1 Turning slightly to the left, LF back in Fallaway Position, turning lady to her right.

Lady's steps

4 LF, still turning to left to face partner.

3 RF to the side to start the Chassé, starting to turn to the left.

2 Replace weight forward to LF.

1 Turning to the right, RF back in Fallaway Position.

Change of Places from Left to Right

This figure will follow the Change of Places from Right to Left, in which the lady turned to her right under the raised arms. She will now turn to her left on the return journey. Again, the lady should not worry about the exact position of her feet as she turns. Follow this figure with the Link Rock. When the preceding Change of Places from Right to Left has been ended with Handshake hold, the Change of Places from Left to Right will be danced with a change of hands. Instead of turning the lady under the joined hands the man will lead the lady to turn to her left with his right hand on step 2, and then release hold immediately. He will catch her right hand in his left hand at the end of her solo turn.

Step 5

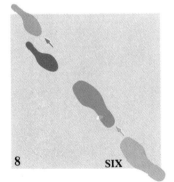

8   SIX

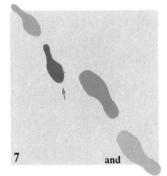

7   and

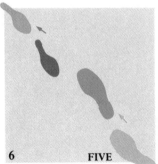

6   FIVE

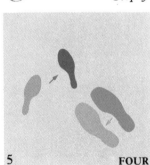

5   FOUR

8 RF. You are now in Open Facing Position.

7 LF, lowering the joined hands.

6 RF forward to start the Chassé still turning the lady to her left.

5 LF, still turning lady to her left.

8 LF. You are now in Open Facing Position; the man will have lowered the joined hands.

7 RF.

6 Still turning slightly to the left to face the man, LF back to start the Chassé.

5 RF, continuing to turn.

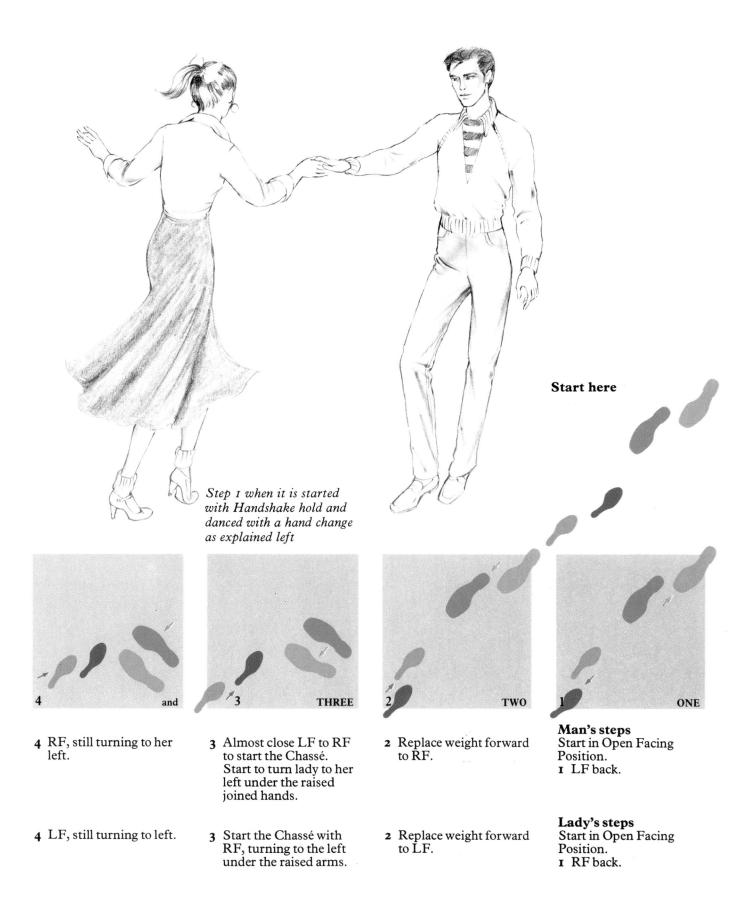

Start here

*Step 1 when it is started
with Handshake hold and
danced with a hand change
as explained left*

4		3		2		1	
	and		THREE		TWO		ONE

4 RF, still turning to her left.

3 Almost close LF to RF to start the Chassé. Start to turn lady to her left under the raised joined hands.

2 Replace weight forward to RF.

Man's steps
Start in Open Facing Position.
1 LF back.

4 LF, still turning to left.

3 Start the Chassé with RF, turning to the left under the raised arms.

2 Replace weight forward to LF.

Lady's steps
Start in Open Facing Position.
1 RF back.

Link Rock

The Link Rock follows the Change of Places from Left to Right, which ends with the partners almost at arm's length away from each other. The Link Rock brings the partners together again. Follow it with the Fallaway Rock.

Step 5

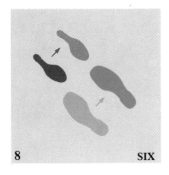

| 8 SIX | 7 and | 6 FIVE | 5 FOUR |

8 RF.

7 LF.

6 RF to the side to start the chassé, taking normal hold.

5 LF.

8 LF.

7 RF.

6 LF to the side to start the Chassé, taking normal hold.

5 RF.

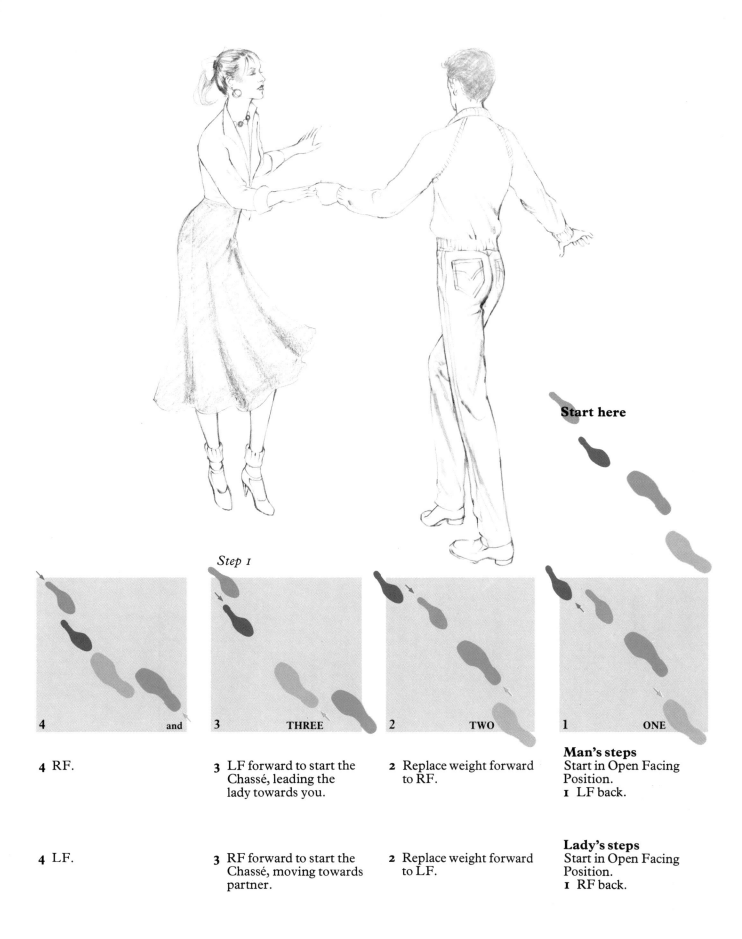

Start here

Step 1

| 4 | and | 3 | THREE | 2 | TWO | 1 | ONE |

4 RF.

3 LF forward to start the Chassé, leading the lady towards you.

2 Replace weight forward to RF.

Man's steps
Start in Open Facing Position.
1 LF back.

4 LF.

3 RF forward to start the Chassé, moving towards partner.

2 Replace weight forward to LF.

Lady's steps
Start in Open Facing Position.
1 RF back.

American Spin

Lead into the American Spin by dancing the Change of Places from Right to Left. At the end of this figure the man puts the lady's right hand into his right hand, and releases hold with his left hand. (This is called the Handshake hold.)

It is important for the man to brace his right arm as he leads the lady towards him, and equally important for the lady to respond with tension

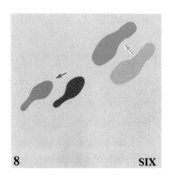

8   SIX

8 RF, taking Handshake hold again at the end of the lady's turn.

8 LF back, having completed half a turn on the Chassé. You are now in Open Facing Position, with Handshake hold again.

End of step 5

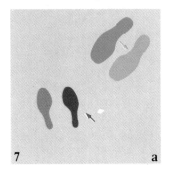

7   a

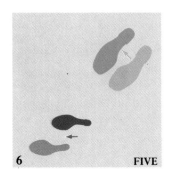

6   FIVE

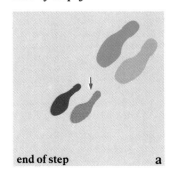

end of step   a

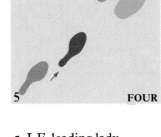

5   FOUR

7 LF.

6 Chassé on the spot starting with RF.

End of step 5
Weight still on left foot.

5 LF, leading lady towards you and bracing your right arm. Then turn lady strongly to her right and release hold.

7 RF, still turning to right.

6 Start the Chassé with LF turning to right.

End of step 5
You are now with your back to the man, with weight still on right foot.

5 RF. Brace right arm and at the end of the step turn a half to the right on RF.

in her right arm – otherwise it will be difficult for the man to spin her. The lady should feel that she is leaning against the man's arm just before she turns.

Repeat the figure. This time the man ends by taking the lady's right hand in his left hand. Follow this second spin with the Change of Places from Left to Right.

Start here

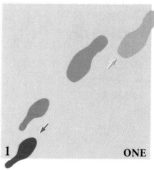

Beginning of step 5

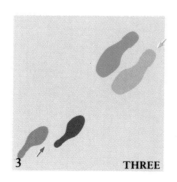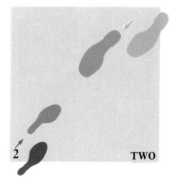

| 4 | 3 | 2 | 1 |
| a | THREE | TWO | ONE |

4 RF, still leading lady forward.

3 Almost close LF to RF as the first step of a Chassé on the spot, starting to lead the lady towards you.

2 Replace weight forward to RF.

Man's steps
Start in Open Facing Position, holding the lady's right hand in your right hand.
1 LF back.

4 LF.

3 RF forward to start the Chassé, moving towards partner. At the end of the last step turn a half to the right on RF to end with back to man.

2 Replace weight forward to LF.

Lady's steps
Start in Open Facing Position, your right hand in man's right hand.
1 RF back.

Suggestions for joining the figures together

1. Fallaway Rock
   Change of Places from Right to Left
   Change of Places from Left to Right
   Link Rock.
2. Change of Places from Right to Left, ending with Handshake hold.
   American Spin, with man catching lady's right hand in his left hand at the end of her spin.
   Change of Places from Left to Right
   Link Rock
   Fallaway Rock.
3. Change of Places from Right to Left. Instead of turning the lady under raised arms, the man releases hold completely at the end of step 5, and the lady does a solo turn.
   Take Handshake hold at the end of the lady's turn.
   Two American Spins. Take Handshake hold again at the end of each spin.
   Change of Places from Left to Right, releasing hold completely at the end of step 2, lady dancing a solo turn.
   Link Rock.

All these groups of figures can be repeated continuously.

How to improve your Jive

Try to develop a rhythmic use of the knees. Dance a series of steps on the same spot, doing each step very firmly on the ball of the foot, then lowering the heel immediately. As you do a step with one foot, relax the knees and say 'One', then straighten the knees very slightly and say 'a'. As you do the step with the other foot, repeat the knee movements, saying, 'Two . . . a'. Carry on to 'Three a', 'Four a', then start over again and keep repeating the steps until you feel you have a slightly springy feeling in the knees. Never straighten the knees stiffly. Try not to bounce but to feel instead that, as you take each step, you are pressing the floor down.

Next, try to retain this springy action as you practise the figures.

It is not necessary to lower the heels on every step. It would be difficult to do so on the first two steps of a Chassé danced at speed.

Points to Remember

More animation is gained on the first step of the Fallaway Rock or Change of Places from Right to Left if the man turns the lady to her right quite strongly. In this way, a full V shape will be obtained for the Promenade Position.

The man should raise the arm high when he is turning the lady under their joined arms, so that she does not bump her head! Unless the lady is turning under the arms, the joined hands should be kept at

Step 2 of Fallaway Rock or Change of Places from Right to Left : lady's side view

Step 5 of American Spin just before lady starts to spin

about her waist level throughout the figure.

The lady should keep her knees quite close together when she is turning on the American Spin. This helps make the spin look neat and controlled.

When the partners end a figure at arm's length from each other, the arms should not straighten completely or they will feel a tug as they step back.

Lady turning under arms on Change of Places from Right to Left

Step 1 of Link Rock or Change of Places from Left to Right

Step 6 of American Spin

THE SAMBA

The rhythmic and lively Samba usually sets feet tapping. It is difficult to stay off the dance floor but not difficult to learn the dance. The music is played at about 48–56 bars a minute, and there are two beats to the bar. The first four figures described – the Reverse Basic Movement, the Whisks, the Walks in Promenade Position and the Reverse Turn – all have the same count: three steps to two beats of music. You count, 'One a Two', taking three quarters of a beat on the first step, a quarter of a beat on the second and whole beat on the third. When you are counting, make the 'a' sound short, to help you take a quicker step. A characteristic of the Samba is the slight bounce, which gives the dance a great deal of animation. The bounce is achieved through flexing and straightening the knees. To practice it, stand with your feet together and knees slightly flexed.

	Say
Straighten your knees very slightly	a
Flex your knees very slightly	One
Straighten your knees very slightly	a
Flex your knees very slightly	Two

Keep doing this, preferably to music, until you do not have to think about it. It will help if you imagine that at the same time you are bouncing a ball on the floor. You use this little bounce on all the figures. Straighten the knees slightly as you start the first step, then flex them slightly as you take your weight on to the foot for count 'One'. Straighten them as you start the next step for count 'a', then flex them again as you take the step for count 'Two'.

Each step danced on the 'a' count is taken on the ball of the foot without lowering the heel. All other steps are started on the ball of the foot and – unless stated otherwise – immediately lowered to the heel. The hold is the normal Latin American hold, as shown on page 69. The dance takes the partners a short distance around the floor.

Reverse Basic Movement

The Reverse Basic Movement is used as a link between the figures. If you wish, you can dance it with a gradual turn – which should never be more than a quarter turn on the complete figure.

On steps 3 and 6 both heels may be lowered, if this feels more comfortable.

Repeat the figure for practice. You may start facing any direction in the room.

Step 1

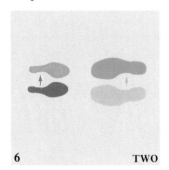 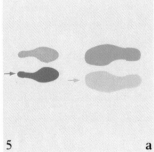

6 TWO	5 a	4 ONE
6 Replace weight to RF and slightly relax the knees (on ball of foot, then flat).	**5** Close LF to RF and slightly straighten the knees (on ball of foot).	**4** RF back and slightly relax the knees (on ball of foot, then lower to heel).
6 Replace weight to LF and slightly relax the knees (on ball of foot, then flat).	**5** Close RF to LF and slightly straighten the knees (on ball of foot).	**4** LF forward and slightly relax the knees (on ball of foot first, then flat).

Step 1, as foot begins to move

Start here

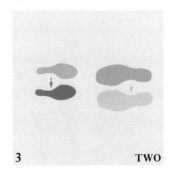

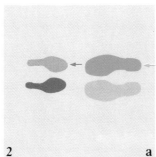

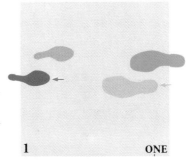

3   **TWO**

2   **a**

1   **ONE**

Man's steps

3 Replace weight to LF and slightly relax the knees (on ball of foot, then flat).

2 Close RF to LF and slightly straighten the knees (on the ball of foot).

1 LF forward and slightly relax the knees (on ball of foot first, then flat).

Lady's steps

3 Replace weight to RF and slightly relax the knees (on ball of foot, then flat).

2 Close LF to RF and slightly straighten the knees (on ball of foot).

1 RF back and slightly relax the knees (on ball of foot, then lower to heel).

Whisks

Dance two Reverse Basic Movements, then dance a Whisk to the left and a Whisk to the right. Repeat the two Whisks and then go into the Reverse Basic Movement again.

Note that the back heel is well clear of the floor on the second step of each Whisk.

WHISK   TO RIGHT

Back view of lady on step 2   **Start here**

3 **TWO**	**2** **a**	**1** **ONE**

3 Replace weight to RF (on ball of foot, then flat).

2 Place left toe behind right heel, LF slightly turned out (on toe).

Man's steps
Start by facing the wall.
1 RF to the side (on ball of foot, then flat).

3 Replace weight to LF (on ball of foot, then flat).

2 Place right toe behind left heel, RF slightly turned out (on toe).

Lady's steps
Start with the back to the wall.
1 LF to the side (on ball of foot, then flat).

WHISK   TO LEFT

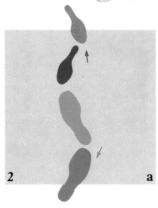

Step 2

Start here

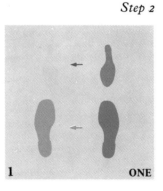

3   **TWO**

2   **a**

1   **ONE**

3 Replace weight to LF (on ball of foot, then flat).

2 Place right toe behind left heel, RF slightly turned out (on toe).

Man's steps
Start by facing the wall.
1 LF to the side (on ball of foot, then flat).

3 Replace weight to RF (on ball of foot, then flat).

2 Place left toe behind right heel, LF slightly turned out (on toe).

Lady's steps
Start with the back to the wall.
1 RF to the side (on ball of foot, then flat).

103

Walks in Promenade Position

Dance four Whisks, the man having started with his left foot. On step 2 of the last Whisk, the man must begin to turn to the left and start to turn the lady to her right, to reach the Promenade Position shown in the illustration. You are now ready to dance the Walks, moving along the line of dance.

Dance four Walks in Promenade Position, then turn inwards to face each other as you dance a Whisk to the left. Continue with three more Whisks.

Keep the front foot quite flat as you pull it back on the third step of each walk.

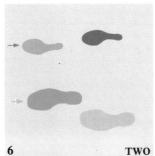 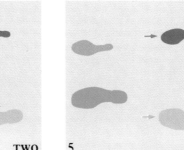 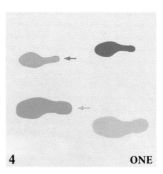

6 TWO	**5** a	**4** ONE
6 Draw RF back about two inches (flat).	**5** LF back, small step (on toe).	**4** RF forward in Promenade Position (on ball of foot, then flat).
6 Draw LF back about two inches (flat).	**5** RF back, small step (on toe).	**4** LF forward in Promenade Position (on ball of foot first, then flat).

104

Front view of starting position

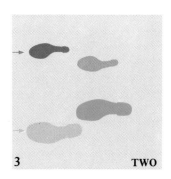

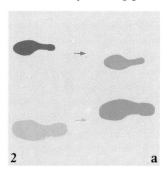

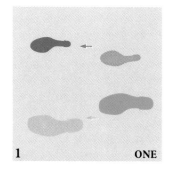

| 3 | TWO | 2 | a | 1 | ONE |

3 Draw LF back about two inches (flat).

2 RF back, small step (on toe).

Man's steps
Start in Promenade Position after a Whisk.
1 LF forward in Promenade Position (on ball of foot, then flat).

3 Draw RF back about two inches (flat).

2 LF back, small step (on toe).

Lady's steps
Start in Promenade Position after a Whisk.
1 RF forward in Promenade Position (on ball of foot first, then flat).

Reverse Turn

Do a Reverse Basic Movement with the man facing the line of dance, and you are now ready to dance a Reverse Turn.

The man should incline his body very slightly to the left on steps 2 and 3 and to the right on steps 5 and 6, while the lady will incline to the right on 2 and 3 and to the left on 5 and 6.

Follow the figure with another Reverse Basic Movement.

Step 3, showing the man's back view

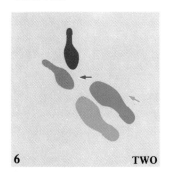 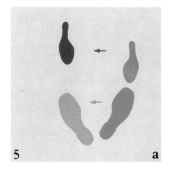 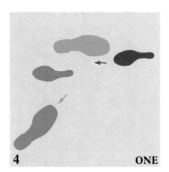

6 Close RF to LF, facing diagonally to the wall (on ball of foot, then flat).

6 Still turning, cross LF well in front of RF with toe of LF turned out, backing diagonally to the wall (on ball of foot, then flat).

5 Still turning, close left heel near to right heel, LF pointing diagonally to the wall (on ball of foot).

5 Still turning, RF to the side and slightly back, backing to the wall (on ball of foot).

4 Still turning, RF back and slightly to the right, backing diagonally to the centre (on ball of foot, then lower to heel).

4 LF forward, turning to the left to face the line of dance (on ball of foot, then flat).

Step 1

Start here

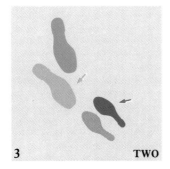

3	**TWO**

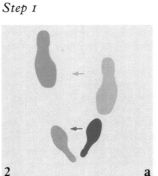

2	**a**

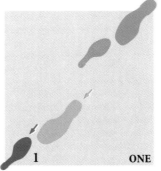

1	**ONE**

3 Still turning, cross LF well in front of RF with toe of LF turned out (on ball of foot, then flat).

3 Close RF to LF, facing diagonally to the wall (on ball of foot, then flat).

2 Still turning to the left, RF to the side and slightly back, backing to the wall (on ball of foot).

2 Still turning to the left, close left heel near to right heel, LF pointing diagonally to the wall (on ball of foot).

Man's steps
Start by facing the line of dance.

1 LF forward, turning to the left, to face diagonally to the centre (on ball of foot, then flat).

Lady's steps
Start with the back to the line of dance.

1 RF back, turning to the left, to back diagonally to the centre (on ball of foot, then lower to heel).

107

Volta Movements

Start with the man facing the wall and dance a Whisk to the Left and a Whisk to the Right. For the Volta Movement, the man moves a little apart from the lady, by sliding his right hand down on to her upper left arm, between her shoulder and elbow; this allows more room to place one foot in front of the other on steps 1, 3, 5 and 7.

Dance a Volta Movement Travelling to the Man's Right, then a Whisk to the Right, a Whisk to the Left, a Volta Movement Travelling to the Man's Left, and finally a Reverse Basic Movement.

Starting position

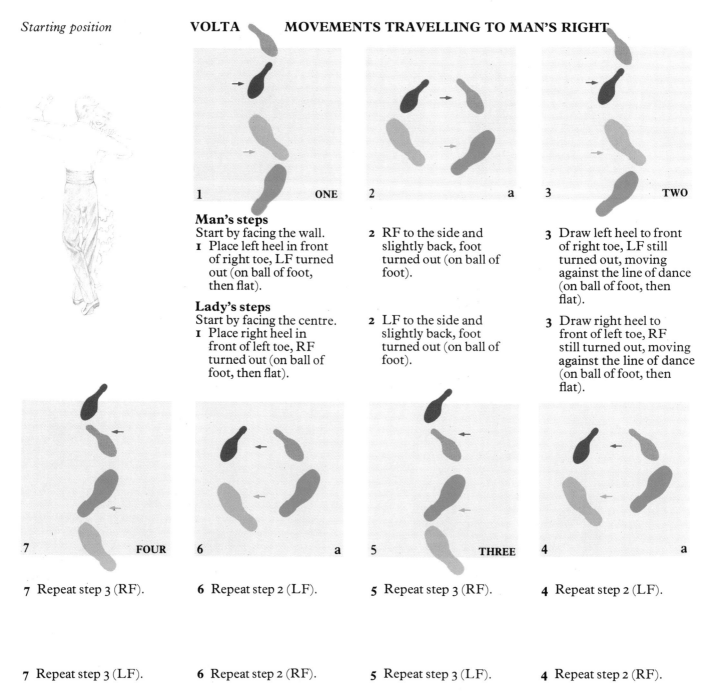

VOLTA MOVEMENTS TRAVELLING TO MAN'S RIGHT

1 ONE

Man's steps
Start by facing the wall.
1 Place left heel in front of right toe, LF turned out (on ball of foot, then flat).

Lady's steps
Start by facing the centre.
1 Place right heel in front of left toe, RF turned out (on ball of foot, then flat).

2 a

2 RF to the side and slightly back, foot turned out (on ball of foot).

2 LF to the side and slightly back, foot turned out (on ball of foot).

3 TWO

3 Draw left heel to front of right toe, LF still turned out, moving against the line of dance (on ball of foot, then flat).

3 Draw right heel to front of left toe, RF still turned out, moving against the line of dance (on ball of foot, then flat).

7 FOUR

7 Repeat step 3 (RF).

7 Repeat step 3 (LF).

6 a

6 Repeat step 2 (LF).

6 Repeat step 2 (RF).

5 THREE

5 Repeat step 3 (RF).

5 Repeat step 3 (LF).

4 a

4 Repeat step 2 (LF).

4 Repeat step 2 (RF).

The illustrated starting position for the Volta Travelling to Man's Right shows clearly the position of steps 1, 3, 5 and 7 of the Volta Travelling to Man's Left. In the same way, the illustrated starting position for the Volta Travelling to Man's Left shows the position of steps 1, 3, 5 and 7 of the Volta Travelling to Man's Right.

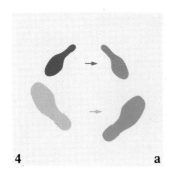 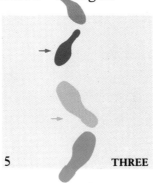 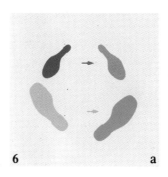 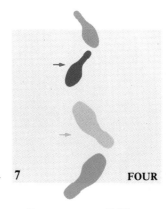

| 4 a | 5 THREE | 6 a | 7 FOUR |

4 Repeat step 2 (RF).

5 Repeat step 3 (LF).

6 Repeat step 2 (RF).

7 Repeat step 3 (LF).

4 Repeat step 2 (LF).

5 Repeat step 3 (RF).

6 Repeat step 2 (LF).

7 Repeat step 3 (RF).

VOLTA MOVEMENTS TRAVELLING TO MAN'S LEFT

Starting position

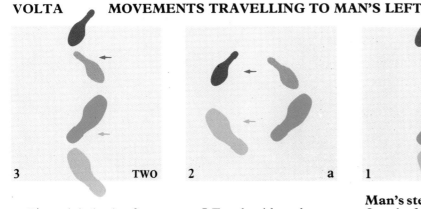

3 Draw right heel to front of left toe, RF still turned out, moving along the line of dance (on ball of foot, then flat).

3 Draw left heel to front of right toe, LF still turned out, moving along the line of dance (on ball of foot, then flat).

2 LF to the side and slightly back, foot turned out (on ball of foot).

2 RF to the side and slightly back, foot turned out (on ball of foot).

Man's steps
Start by facing the wall.
1 Place right heel in front of left toe, RF turned out (on ball of foot, then flat).

Lady's steps
Start by facing the centre.
1 Place left heel in front of right toe, LF turned out (on ball of foot, then flat).

109

Suggestions for joining the figures together

1 Start with the man facing the wall
  2 Reverse Basic Movements (no turn)
  4 Whisks, man starting with left foot and partners turning to Promenade Position on the last Whisk
  4 Walks in Promenade Position, man starting with left foot
  4 Whisks, man (starting with left foot) turning to right and lady turning to left to face each other on the first step.
2 Start with the man facing the wall
  2 Reverse Basic Movements, turning a quarter to left so that the man faces the line of dance
  Reverse Turn
  Repeat the Reverse Turn, the man taking the first step down the line of dance and ending by facing the wall
  4 Whisks, man starting with left foot
  Volta Movement, man travelling to right
  2 Whisks, man starting with right foot
  Volta Movement, man travelling to left.

These groups of figures can be repeated continuously.

How to improve your Samba

Try to remember that the beat value of each set of three steps in the first four figures is: three quarters of a beat, a quarter of a beat and a whole beat. Coming after the second, quick step, the third step will seem comparatively slow, and there is often a tendency to hurry it, this spoiling the rhythmic feeling of the dance. To counteract this, you may find it helpful while doing the step to say, instead of 'One a two', 'One a step', prolonging the sound of 'step'.

Keep the slight bouncing action you have learned to a minimum on the Walks in Promenade Position.

As you become more proficient, try curving the Volta movements. For example, in group of figures 2, curve a quarter turn to the left on the first Volta Movement (as man travels to the Right), ending with the man facing the line of dance, and curve a quarter turn to the right on the second Volta Movement (as man travels to the left), ending with the man facing the wall again.

Points to Remember

Do not exaggerate the bounce. The straightening and flexing of the knees should be very slight.

Keep your steps small. Although the dance is designed to move around the floor, the progression is slight and gradual.

Do not forget that the Reverse Basic Movement may be turned. Use it between figures as many times as needed to achieve the desired starting alignment for the next step.

Walks to Promenade Position (man starting with right foot): step 1

Step 2 of Whisk to Left

Step 2

Step 3. These three steps all show the lady's side view

Starting to move into Walk in Promenade Position (man starting with left foot)

——THE——
RUMBA

The Rumba is the most graceful of the Latin American dances. Rumba music is played at about 28–31 bars a minute, and each bar has four beats. To each four beats you dance three steps. The first and second steps each take one beat, the third step takes two beats. This timing is constant throughout the figures described. Listen carefully to the music and you will hear the beats – one, two, three, four. Each figure starts on the second beat of the bar: a characteristic of the dance is that there is no movement of the feet on beat one, just a movement of the hips. As in the Cha Cha Cha, every step is started on the ball of the foot, with the knee flexed. As weight is taken on to the foot, the heel is lowered to the floor and the knee straightened. The other knee is then slightly flexed, with the heel just off the floor. The hips swing naturally to the same side as the stepping foot.

Practise this exercise to help you with the rhythmic action. First, stand with your feet a little apart and take your weight on to the left foot, allowing the hips to move to the left. The left leg should be straight, the knee of the other leg relaxed, with the heel slightly off the floor. Now imagine you are waiting for a train and your left leg is getting tired – so change your weight to the right foot and allow the hips to move to the right. Now change the weight to the left foot again, and keep repeating the movements. Now try the exercise while counting the beat. First, stand with your weight on the left foot.

	Say
Change weight to right foot, moving hips to right (preliminary movement, before steps are taken).	One
	Two
Change weight to left foot, moving hips to left.	
Change weight to right foot, moving hips to right	Three
Change weight to left foot, moving hips slowly to left	Four, One
Change weight to right foot, moving hips to right	Two
	Three
Change weight to left foot, moving hips to left	
Change weight to right foot, moving hips slowly to right.	Four, One

Practise this exercise until you can do it naturally. When you have learned the pattern of a figure, try to introduce the action into the figure. When you are ready to start take the normal Latin hold as shown on page 69. Stand in the position you have learned for the exercise, the man with his weight on the left foot, the lady with her weight on the right. When you hear the first beat of a bar change your weight to the other foot. You are now ready to take the first step of the Basic Movement on the second beat. In the Rumba you do not move around the floor, so you may start your figures facing in any direction.

Basic Movement

You will find it easier to learn the steps without turning. After you have mastered the pattern and can dance it successfully to music, try turning very gradually to the left. Do not make more than a quarter of a turn to the left over the six steps.

Repeat the Basic Movement as many times as you wish.

Step 4

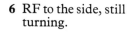

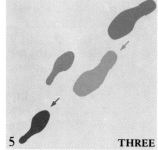

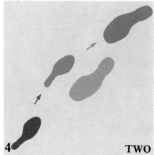

6 RF to the side, still turning.

5 Replace weight forward to LF, still turning.

4 RF back.

6 LF to the side and slightly back, still turning.

5 Replace weight back to RF.

4 LF forward, still turning.

114

Step 3

Start here

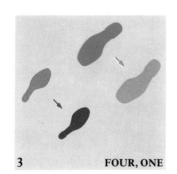

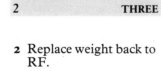

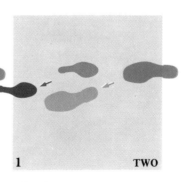

| 3 | FOUR, ONE | 2 | THREE | 1 | TWO |

Man's steps

3 LF to the side and slightly back, still turning slightly.

2 Replace weight back to RF.

1 LF forward, starting to turn to the left.

Lady's steps

3 RF to the side, still turning slightly.

2 Replace weight forward to LF, starting to turn to the left.

1 RF back.

Fan

Dance a Basic Movement to lead into the Fan.

On step 5 of the Fan, the man must help the lady turn away from him with a little guidance from his right hand on her back before he releases the hold.

Follow the figure with the Alemana.

Step 5

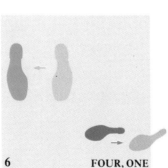

6   FOUR, ONE

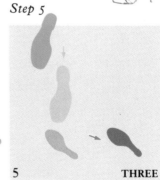

5   THREE

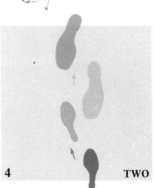

4   TWO

6 RF to the side. You are now in the Fan Position as illustrated on page 119 overleaf.

6 LF back, still turning slightly, to end in the Fan Position on partner's left side as illustrated on page 119 overleaf.

5 Replace weight forward to LF, helping the lady to turn to her left with your right hand before releasing hold with it.

5 RF back and slightly to the right, still turning to the left and moving away from partner. (The man has released hold of your left hand).

4 RF back, turning the lady very slightly to her left.

4 LF forward, turning very slightly to left.

116

Step 2

Start here

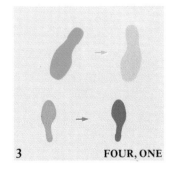

3   **FOUR, ONE**

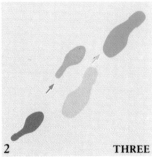

2   **THREE**

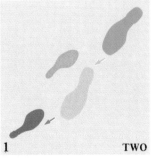

1   **TWO**

Man's steps

1 LF forward, starting to turn to the left.

2 Replace weight back to RF.

3 LF to the side and slightly back, still turning slightly to the left.

Lady's steps

1 RF back.

2 Replace weight forward to LF, starting to turn to the left.

3 RF to the side, still turning.

Alemana

Having danced the Fan, you are now in position to do the Alemana.

It is important for the man to lead well. On steps 2 and 3 he must guide the lady forward with his left hand, and also on step 3 he must raise his left arm, starting to turn the lady to the right with a clockwise movement of his left hand. The normal hold should be resumed at the end of the last step.

Follow the Alemana with the Basic Movement.

Step 3

6 FOUR, ONE	5 THREE	4 TWO
6 Close RF to LF, and resume normal hold.	**5** Replace weight forward to LF, still turning the lady.	**4** RF back, turning the lady to her right under the raised arms.
6 LF forward, still turning to face partner and resume normal hold.	**5** RF forward, still turning.	**4** LF forward, turning to the right under raised arms (the man has raised your right arm).

Starting position

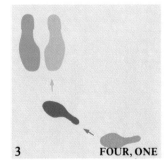

3   FOUR, ONE

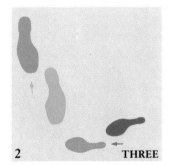

2   THREE

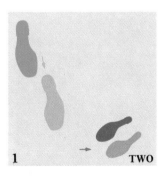

1   TWO

Start here

3 Close LF to RF, still leading the lady forward, at the same time raising your left arm and starting to turn the lady to her right.

3 RF forward, starting to turn to the right.

2 Replace weight back to RF, leading the lady forward.

2 LF forward.

Man's steps
Start in Fan Position.
1 LF forward.

Lady's steps
Start in Fan Position.
1 Close RF to LF.

119

Hand to Hand and Spot Turn

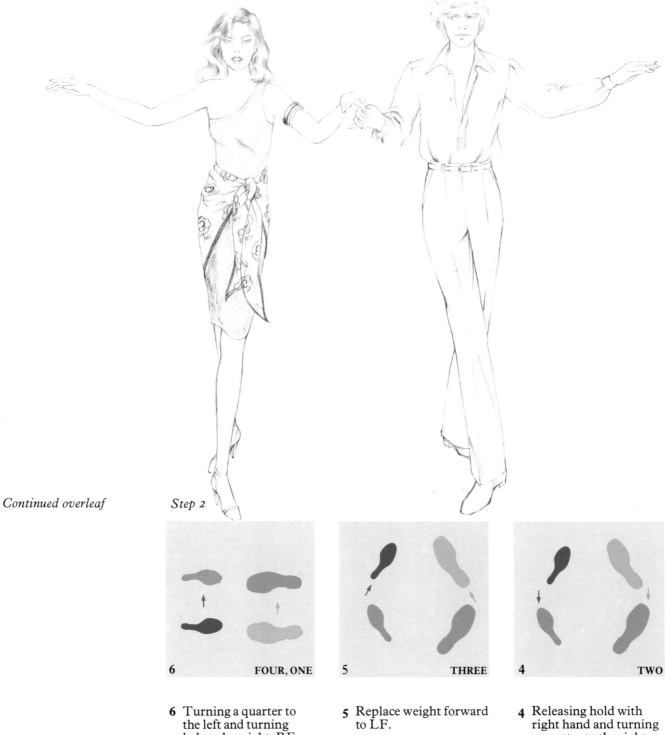

Continued overleaf

Step 2

6 FOUR, ONE	5 THREE	4 TWO

6 Turning a quarter to the left and turning lady to her right, RF to the side. Now facing lady again, take her left hand in your right.

5 Replace weight forward to LF.

4 Releasing hold with right hand and turning a quarter to the right, RF back, turning lady to her left.

6 Turning a quarter to the right, LF to the side, facing partner, who has taken your left hand in his right hand again.

5 Replace weight forward to RF.

4 Turning a quarter to the left, LF back (man has released hold of your left hand).

First dance the Fan and Alemana. To start the new figure, both partners take the last step of the Alemana to the side and at the same time take the double hand hold as illustrated.

Steps 1–9 form the Hand to Hand; steps 10–12 are the Spot Turn.

Keep the arms steady throughout steps 1–9. This, coupled with the man's turn, should provide a sufficient lead for the lady.

On step 9, the man does not take the lady's right hand in his left hand again. Instead, he must, with his right hand, help her start her Spot Turn to the right, then release hold with his right hand.

Resume the normal hold at the end of the Spot Turn and go into the Basic Movement.

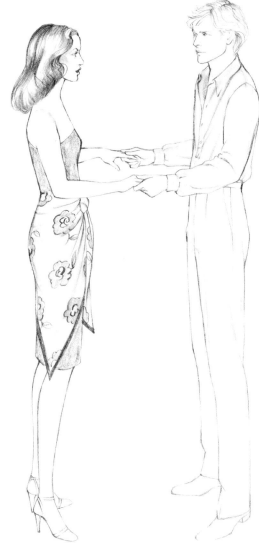

Starting position

Start here

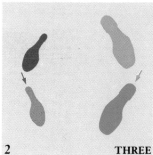

| 3 FOUR | 2 THREE | 1 TWO |

3 Turning a quarter to the right and turning lady to her left, LF to the side. Now facing lady again, take her right hand in your left.

2 Replace weight forward to RF.

1 Releasing hold with your left hand and turning a quarter to the left, LF back, turning lady to her right.

Man's steps
Start by facing partner, a little apart from her and holding both her hands.

3 Turning a quarter to the left, RF to the side, facing partner, who has taken your right hand in his left hand again.

2 Replace weight forward to LF.

1 Turning a quarter to the right, RF back (man has released hold of your right hand).

Lady's steps
Start by facing partner, a little apart from him and holding both his hands.

121

Starting to take normal hold on step 12

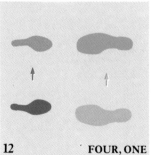

| 12 | FOUR, ONE | 11 | THREE |

12 Turning a further quarter to the left to face partner again, RF to the side and resume normal hold.

11 Turn a half to the left on RF, keeping LF in place, and transfer weight forward to LF.

12 Turning a further quarter to the right to face partner again, LF to the side and resume normal hold.

11 Turn a half to the right on LF keeping RF in place, and transfer weight forward to RF.

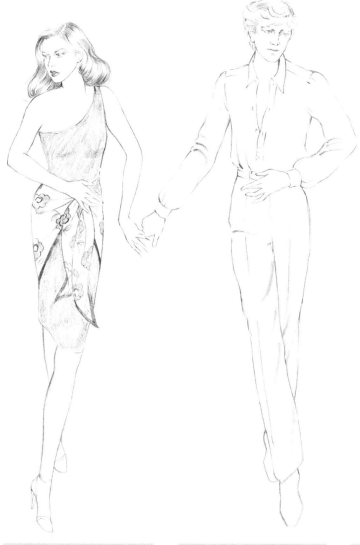

Step 10

Continued from previous page

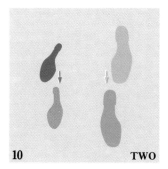

10   **TWO**

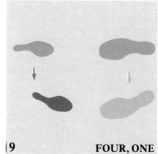

9   **FOUR, ONE**

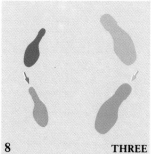

8   **THREE**

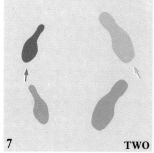

7   **TWO**

Man's steps

7 Repeat step 1 (LF).

10 Completing a quarter turn to the left, RF forward, releasing hold with right hand.

9 Repeat step 3 (LF). At the end of the step, start to turn to the left and start to turn lady to her right.

8 Repeat Step 2 (RF).

Lady's steps

7 Repeat step 1 (RF)

10 Completing a quarter turn to the right, LF forward. Man releases hold of your left hand.

9 Repeat step 3 (RF). At the end of the step, start to turn to the right.

8 Repeat step 2 (LF).

Suggestions for joining the figures together

1 Basic Movement
Fan
Alemana.

2 Fan
Alemana, man and lady ending to side and taking double hand hold
Hand to Hand
Spot Turn, resuming normal hold at the end (man turning left, lady right)
Basic Movement.

3 Fan
Alemana, man and lady ending to side and taking double hand hold
Steps 1–6 of the Hand to Hand, resuming normal hold at the end of step 6
Basic Movement.

4 Steps 1–3 of Basic Movement, man releasing hold with right hand at end of step 3
Steps 4–9 of Hand to Hand
Spot Turn (man turning right, lady left)
Basic Movement.

All these groups of figures can be repeated continuously.

How to improve your Rumba
To develop a rhythmic feeling and action, practise the Basic Movement with the music played as slowly as possible and, as you take your steps, counting, 'Two and, Three and, Four One and'. Do not allow the hips to complete their journey until you say the 'and'. In this way you will be using the beat of the music to achieve continuous motion.

When the man is leading the lady to the Fan Position he should feel as he takes step 4 that his arms are moving in slightly towards his body. As the lady moves away, the partners should slowly extend their free arm to the side just below shoulder level; it should not be moved abruptly but arrive in position at the same time as the last step. Study the illustrations showing this.

When dancing the Spot Turn, the partners should look at each other before they start the turn and again as they complete the turn (see illustration far right).

Points to Remember
Feel that you are pressing the ball of the foot into the floor as you take every step. Also press the ball of the front foot into the floor at the end of every backward step.

Never let the ball of the foot leave the floor.

Arm movements should be gentle and the hands should be used gracefully, with the fingers kept close but not tightly, together.

Step 3 of Alemana

Step 1 of Hand to Hand

Step 4 of Fan

Moving into step 6 of Fan

Step 4 of Hand to Hand

Step 9 of Hand to Hand before starting Spot Turn

THE
PASO DOBLE

This is an exciting dance based on the Spanish bull fight: the man represents the matador and the lady his cape. At an advanced level, the arm movements become fairly difficult as the man flourishes his 'cape' to make the various passes used in the bull ring. However, at a social level, the dance is quite easy to learn. The stirring music is played at about 60–62 bars a minute, and there are two beats to the bar. It is 'marching' music, and you will distinctly hear the steady 'One, two, one, two', inviting you to march 'Right, left, right, left'. Each step takes one beat of music, and you cannot fail to keep time. Although the dance originated in Spain, it was the French who developed it into a social dance. This explains the name of the first figure, Sur Place, meaning 'in place' or 'on the spot'. This figure is simply a series of marking-time steps danced on the balls of the feet.

Practise it as your first exercise. Stand with your feet together and step first on one foot and then the other. The man should start with his right foot, the lady with her left, as this is what happens in every figure. Imagine you are stepping without shoes on wet sand. Try hard to squeeze the water out of the sand with the ball of your foot on each step. Do not bend your knees – although they must be relaxed, not stiff. Now practise the exercise to music, taking one step to each beat, and saying, 'One, two, one, two'. Try to sense a feeling of strength in your feet and ankles, and dance every step that is taken on the ball of the foot with this feeling. The other steps of the Paso Doble are easy, marching steps forward, danced heel first. The hold for the Paso Doble is shown on page 69. It is up to you whether you stand a little apart, as in the other Latin American dances, or close, as in the ballroom hold. Try to take up a proud, upright stance. Make yourself as tall as possible, but at the same time keep your shoulders relaxed.

Chassé to Right

Lead into the Chassé to Right by dancing eight steps of Sur Place with the man facing the centre. Dance four Chassés, and follow them with eight steps of Sur Place.

The heels may be lowered during the Chassés. You may dance any number of Chassés although two or four is usually most practical. The Chassés may be gradually turned to the left or the right to achieve a position in the room from which to dance the next figure. Two alternative methods of dancing the Chassés would be to dance them very high on the toes, or with the feet flat and the knees slightly flexed. An attractive combination would be to dance two Chassés on the toes and two flat.

Step 1

Start here

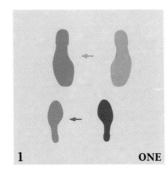

2 | TWO

1 | ONE

2 Close LF to RF (ball of foot).

Man's steps
Start by facing the centre.
1 RF to the side (ball of foot).

2 Close RF to LF (ball of foot).

Lady's steps
Start with the back to the centre.
1 LF to the side (ball of foot).

Sur Place

This is a series of marking-time steps danced on the spot, replacing the weight from one foot to the other. It is danced on the balls of the feet, although the heels may just touch the floor. The Sur Place is used to link figures together and its simple steps give partners plenty of time to think what they are going to do next. It is usual to dance a series of four or eight steps, one step to each beat of music. The figure may be danced without a turn or turned to right or left.

Forward Basic Movement

Like Sur Place, the Forward Basic Movement is used to link figures together and is usually danced in series of four or eight steps. The partners may curve to the right or left, and the heels may be lowered.

Start here

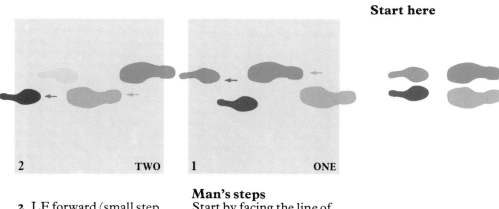

| 2 | TWO | 1 | ONE |

Man's steps
Start by facing the line of dance.
1 RF forward (small step on ball of foot).

2 LF forward (small step on ball of foot).

Lady's steps
Start with the back to the line of dance.
1 LF back (small step on ball of foot).

2 RF back (small step on ball of foot).

Separation

The man should start to lead the lady away from him on step 2 by lowering his arms a little and extending them slightly forward. He should extend the left arm still further when he releases hold with the right hand on step 3. He should lead the lady back to him on steps 5–8 by gradually drawing his left arm back to its starting position.

Dance four or eight steps of Sur Place before and after the Separation.

Man's steps

5–8 Four Sur Place RF, LF, RF, LF, gradually leading lady towards you. Take normal hold again on last step.

Lady's steps

5–8 Four small steps forward, LF, RF, LF, RF, gradually moving towards man. Take normal hold again on last step.

Step 3

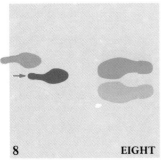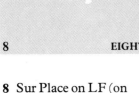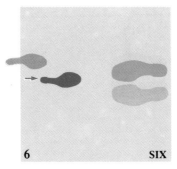

8 EIGHT	7 SEVEN	6 SIX	5 FIVE

8 Sur Place on LF (on ball of foot).

7 Close RF to LF, still leading lady back and releasing hold with right hand (on balls of both feet).

6 LF forward, leading lady to take a long step back (heel first).

Man's steps

Start by facing the line of dance in this position.

5 Firmly step on the spot with RF, slightly bending the knees (foot flat).

Lady's steps

Start with back to line of dance in this position.

5 Firmly step on the spot with LF, slightly bending the knees (foot flat).

8 Close RF to LF (on balls of both feet).

7 LF back (on ball of foot). Man has released hold with his right hand.

6 RF back (long step on ball of foot, then lowering heel).

130

Promenade Link

Lead into the Promenade Link by dancing four steps of Sur Place with the man facing the line of dance.

This figure can also be started with the man facing the wall; when danced in this way, the man would finish by facing the line of dance.

Note the position of the arms when the partners are in the Promenade Position.

Follow the figure with Sur Place or Chassés to the right.

Start here

Step 3

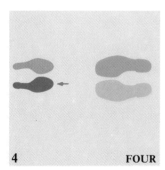 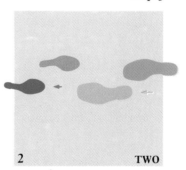 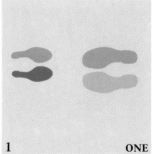

4 FOUR	3 THREE	2 TWO	1 ONE

4 Close LF to RF, facing centre and turning lady to face you (flat, or on balls of both feet).

3 Turning slightly to the left, RF forward and across LF in Promenade Position and pointing to the centre (heel first).

2 Turning slightly to the left, LF to the side in Promenade Position and pointing diagonally to the centre (heel first).

Man's steps
Start by facing the line of dance.
1 Firmly step on the spot with RF, slightly bending the knees (foot flat).

4 Still turning to the left on LF, close RF to LF, facing the wall (on balls of both feet).

3 LF forward in Promenade Position starting to turn to the left (heel first).

2 Turning slightly to the right, RF to the side in Promenade Position with the back diagonally to the wall (heel first).

Lady's steps
Start with the back to the line of dance.
1 Firmly step on the spot with LF, slightly bending the knees (foot flat).

131

Suggestions for joining the figures together

Throughout the groups of figures count consistently from 1 to 8.

		Count
1	Start with the man facing the line of dance	
	4 Forward Basic Movements	1–4
	4 steps of Sur Place turning to left so that man faces the centre	5–8
	4 Chassés to Right	1–8
	4 steps of Sur Place turning to right so that man faces the line of dance	1–4
	4 steps of Sur Place without turning.	5–8
2	Start with the man facing the line of dance	
	4 steps of Sur Place without turning	1–4
	Promenade Link	5–8
	2 Chassés to Right	1–4
	4 steps of Sur Place turning to right so that man faces the line of dance.	5–8
3	Start with the man facing the line of dance	
	4 Forward Basic Movements	1–4
	4 steps of Sur Place without turning	5–8
	Separation	1–8
	Separation may be repeated.	
4	Start with the man facing the line of dance	
	Separation	1–8
	4 steps of Sur Place without turning	1–4
	Promenade Link	5–8
	2 Chassés to Right	1–4
	4 steps of Sur Place turning to right so that man faces the line of dance.	5–8
5	Start with the man facing the wall	
	Promenade Link	1–4
	(Man is now facing the line of dance.)	
	2 Chassés to Right, moving towards the wall	5–8
	Separation	1–8

Groups of figures 1–4 can be repeated continuously.

How to improve your Paso Doble

Each step should be crisp and firm. Try to take the step sharply at the beginning of the beat and, when you are dancing the small steps, as in Sur Place, Forward Basic Movement and Chassé to Right, hold the position momentarily at the end of the beat. Say 'step, stop' to yourself as you dance each step.

The first step of the Promenade Link and the Separation is known as the Appel; this is a 'call to the bull' and should be taken very firmly, rather like a silent stamp.

As you turn to Promenade Position in the Promenade Link, widen the hold a little. Lower and extend the joined arms to just below chest level. They should be gently curved.

The Separation can be made more expressive if you rise very high to the toes on step 4, then gradually lower the heels to the floor over steps 5–8. Do not let the free arm hang loosely in this figure; raise it to the side, slightly curved and below shoulder level.

Points to Remember

Keep the arms firm, but not stiff, at all times. Remember that the Sur Place and Forward Basic Movement act as links between the figures and that you can turn them to right or left. This makes it easy to reach the right position from which to start the next figure.

When you are dancing Chassés to Right near the end of the room (with the man looking towards the centre of the room) you may turn gradually to the left to get around the corner.

Correct hold for Paso Doble

132

Step 1 of Promenade Link, starting to turn to Promenade Position : lady's back view

Step 2 of Promenade Link : lady's side view

Step 1 of Separation

Step 2 of Separation

MEDAL TESTS
AND COMPETITIONS

Dancing not only provides social pleasures. To many people, it is also a worth-while and satisfying hobby, one that can be enjoyed with or without a regular partner.

There is ample opportunity for pupils attending a good dancing school to measure their progress by entering medal tests. These tests are conducted by dancing societies in many parts of the world, and cover ballroom, Latin American and now even disco dancing. There are awards for proficiency at the level of social dancing, followed by bronze, silver and gold medals, and eventually even higher awards. All the awards demand sound technique and rhythm, and they require progressively higher standards of style, movement and control.

A medal test can be taken at any age and with one's own partner, another member of the class, or a teacher. Once you have gained a medal, you can pit yourself against other medallists of your standard. There are competitions that cater for all age groups and levels, for beginners and champions. Many schools enter their pupils for trophies.

In the beginner and novice competitions formal evening dress is not always required, but it becomes obligatory as couples rise to the higher grades. In the Ballroom section, the man needs a well-cut tail suit, and the lady a glamorous dress which will enhance her charm without restricting her movement. Over the years there has been no dramatic change in this Ballroom style. In Latin American competitions most men wear a cat suit, a one-piece outfit in a material that stretches so that the movement of body and arms is not impeded. The lady's dress is usually quite short to reveal her leg action. Latin American styles change considerably, according to the fashion of the moment. Whatever the competition, immaculate grooming is essential for both the man and the lady.

A couple must present a pleasing yet unaffected dancing style. When the floor is crowded, a judge's first impression of a couple will be based on this general style. Many factors contribute to a good style. There must be poise, fluid movement, accurate, well controlled use of the feet, an ability to express the rhythm and character of each dance, and artistry.

One interesting feature of competitions is formation dancing. Several couples – usually three to eight – dance as a team, performing figures in unison to a choreography of lines, circles and intricate patterns. To work as one of a team in this way can be most rewarding and great fun.

Maximum attention is paid to the costume of the teams. The men wear the same type of suit, shirt and tie, and the ladies identical dresses. Details are all very important. The ladies usually have their hair dressed in the same way or wear wigs of the same style and colour. Earrings, shoes and other accessories are matching. The men even have their hair cut to the same length where possible!

Dressing the teams can be costly, so dancing schools which train formation teams often organize fund-raising dances, raffles and other events to help with the expenses. The dancers and their coaches put in many hours of hard work as they strive to attain perfection, usually finding it all worthwhile. To be working as part of a formation team can be most rewarding and great fun.

The Star Professional
Championships 1979.
Previous page : The Latin
American Championship.
Left : Robert and Linda
Bellinger from Southamp-
ton, dancing in the
Ballroom Championship.
This page : Espen and
Kirsten Salberg from
Norway and (inset) Ray
and Deirdre Baker from
Australia, dancing in
the Latin American
Championship.

DISCO DANCING

Disco dancing really began in 1955 when Bill Haley and The Comets released a record called *Rock Around The Clock* – and teenagers all over the world responded with joy to a sound and beat they could call their own. Of course, Mr Haley and his men had not invented the sound. Its origins could be found in 'race music' or 'rhythm and blues' as it was more politely called. This, the music of the American black community, had already become popular on radio shows such as Alan Freed's *Rock and Roll Party*. At the same time, post-war affluence meant that teenagers had money to spend. With the advent of cheap radios and single records, a new youth market began to open up. Recording companies were not slow to realize that the product their new customers could never get enough of was Rock and Roll. It became the private language of the young – a way to express the feelings and desires of a generation of teenagers.

Dancing to Rock and Roll was also a far cry from the sedate Foxtrots and Waltzes performed by one's elders in ballrooms across the nation. For a start, nobody dressed up. There were no special dancing shoes or dresses because most of the dancing took place in high school gyms at lunch time, or in the local hall after school. If you were really lucky and lived in Philadelphia, you could go round to the ABC TV Studios after school and get the chance to appear on *Dick Clark's American Bandstand*. This show, which swept the USA, started life as a cheap summer replacement: just a disc jockey in a bare studio who played records while an assortment of local kids danced. Teenagers all over the country avidly watched the dances performed on the show so that they could be the first in their neighbourhood to have mastered a new step.

The basis for all these variations was a fairly simple dance called the Lindyhop, closely related to the earlier Jive and Jitterbug. Each couple felt called upon to be as inventive and creative as possible with the result that there were almost as many steps as performers. The only exceptions to this style were the 'line dances' – such as the Stroll and the Madison – performed, as the name implies, in long lines of couples facing each other. Even here, although the basic step was repeated over and over, it was possible for each couple to do their own variation when it came to their turn to 'go down the line'. Eventually, dancing became so individual that partners stopped holding hands at all and, although still facing each other, began to dance completely independently. The stage was set for the arrival of Chubby Checker and the Twist.

While the Lindyhop had borne some resemblance to traditional ballroom styles of social dancing in that a couple held hands and moved around the floor, it had also begun to incorporate a lot of extra body movements, using the hips, torso and pelvis. A lot more of the body was being used than had hitherto been thought decorous. With the Twist, decorum went straight out of the window. Dancers found themselves squashed together on very small dance floors, performing the most energetic hip-swinging gyrations and moving their feet very little.

Discotheques (the French name for a night-club where records are played instead of live music) were the setting in which patrons twisted the night away. If, during the evening, you felt the need for inspiration, or just a breather, you could watch the professional 'Go-Go Dancers' hired by many clubs to perform the latest variations on the basic theme. Good Go-Go Dancers not only moved well, but knew the records backwards, which enabled them to improvise with a high degree of subtlety and finesse.

Once people got used to moving on their own, all sorts of new dances were possible. Under the general heading of the Frug, also a dance in which one's feet remained firmly rooted to the floor, whilst everything else rotated, there appeared a steady stream of new crazes. The Jerk, the Hitchhiker, the Swim, and a whole host of dances named after animals: the Alligator, the Monkey, the Dog, the Pony, etc., all with appropriate hand and arm movements. If you could find the space to move your feet just a little bit, you could indulge in the Mashed Potato, using the balls of your feet in a mashing movement; the Slop, a kind of sloppy walking on the spot; or the Watusi, in which you occasionally lifted one knee in between nodding your head violently and using your arms in a pushing gesture.

By the late sixties popular music had taken a more lyrical direction. The Woodstock Generation, the hippies and flower people, were not interested in going to discotheques. If they danced at all, it was likely to be some kind of hand-clapping and jumping, spinning, or head-shaking. People who still wanted to indulge in real dancing rather than random movements found themselves tuning their radios to the local 'soul station' for the music they wanted to hear. Soul music required what was generally known as 'funky dancing', but individual dances were few and seldom named. One exception, of course, was the Funky Chicken, in which the dancers flap their arms like wings, and occasionally mime the strain of laying an egg!

By the mid-seventies, soul music was making its way into the pop charts and along with a general interest in fitness, dancing for pleasure was enjoying a great increase in popularity. People had discovered that dancing was a great way to exercise without the boredom of jogging or calisthenics. Classes for disco dancing sprang up all over the place, mainly held in the late afternoon or early evening, so that office workers and housewives could attend.

After the sixties, when people had nearly always danced as individuals, people again became more interested in dancing with some relationship to each other. The first sign of this was a dance which enjoyed worldwide popularity – the Bump. It was a very simple idea: partners rebounded off each other, using different parts of their bodies, most usually the buttocks! If not done with some expertise, it was possible to miss completely, causing embarrassment, or to inflict injury on one's partner by a too forceful approach. However, it was fun to dance with someone else again, and individuals, perhaps acquaintances from discos or dance classes, began to team up to create and practise their own routines. At the same time, discotheques began sponsoring dance contests which were open to everyone.

The dance most often seen in these contests was The Hustle. This, like most social dances, started with a new sound in music. In the mid-seventies, soul music and jazz began exploring a Latin-American double beat as a backing to the melody, instead of the heavy off-beat which had previously dominated. This sound called for a new kind of movement: something with a more even feel, producing a gentle, lilting quality.

The first Hustles were primarily one or two steps repeated over and over, facing a new direction at each repeat. These could be performed by individuals or couples or incorporated into line dances. Gradually hustles became localized: the New York Hustle or the L.A. Hustle, for example. Even individual discotheques initiated their own versions. Couples worked on their own routines, expanding them to include holds and lifts copied from such different sources as ballet and ballroom dancing. They practised with great diligence and secrecy for competition. Then in 1977, a film called *Saturday Night Fever* appeared and disco dancing really came into its own. The fact that the film was made at all meant that the producers had confidence that its subject, the story

140

of a guy who only lives for his Saturday night at the local disco, would be a winner. Every song in the film became a hit record, and people from Brooklyn to Bangkok caught the fever.

A book about social dancing would now be incomplete without its section on disco dancing. Ballroom dancing associations all over the world have included the new category in their competitions. It is a great way to keep fit, have fun, meet people, and a wonderful way to relax and unwind. It is a true popular folk art form and the possibilities for self-expression and communication are limited only by the skill and imagination of the performers.

On the following pages, some of the most individual disco dances are illustrated and explained. Some of the styles are really up-to-the-minute, others, like the Twist and the Lindyhop, are old favourites still guaranteed to fill the floor the minute the appropriate music is played.

The most important thing to remember about any kind of disco dancing is that it really doesn't matter so much what you do, as how you do it. Most dances are composed of only a few basic moves. They are only the framework on which dancers are meant to improvise. The whole idea of disco dancing is to look good, to show off. Style is all important; the way you perform the steps is much more important than the steps themselves. Usually, if it feels right, it is right.

However, there is one very important point to remember. Some people have a tendency to clap and dance *on* the beat, but no good disco dancer ever dances *on* the beat. It is *off* the beat, the 'and' between 'one' and 'two', which gives good disco dancing its special feeling. After all, most of the music is directly related to jazz.

A good way to become aware of the difference is to try clapping in time to a disco record. First clap on the beat: *one* and *two* and *three* and *four*. Then try clapping off the beat: one *and* two *and* three *and* four. The difference is obvious. Dancing on the beat is moving to the music, going along with it. In dancing off the beat, the dancer becomes a part of the music, using body rhythms to complement the existing beat. Rather like two drums, the dancer and music talk to each other. Even in dances like the Hustle, where the foot patterns are stepped on the beat, the body movements of the hips are on the off-beat – giving the dance its distinctive lilting quality.

Now you're ready to try the dances in the next section. If a full-length mirror is available, practise routines in front of it. It's best to practise in something similar to whatever you are likely to wear at the disco or party, as clothes can either enhance your style, or create problems you'll need to know about. Whether you choose to bop, boogie, bump or bus stop, have a good time.

Rock and Roll

The basic Lindyhop step is the link between traditional forms of ballroom dancing and disco dancing. Partners face each other and take the traditional ballroom dancing position. The girl starts on her right foot and the man on his left. This dance, however, is often performed by two girls, in which case it doesn't matter who takes which side as the movements mirror each other.

The step takes eight counts to complete, made up of the following:
First foot: toe, heel (1, 2)
Second foot: toe, heel (3, 4)
Change to ball of foot, crossing first foot behind (5, 6)
Step on the spot with first foot (7)
Step on the spot with second foot (8)

Once you have mastered the basic step, you and your partner can add breaks, lifts and turns to form a continuous routine. Here are just a few variations, illustrated on the opposite page and overleaf.
Make sure, when trying any of the lifts for the first time, to have people around to 'spot' (catch). A fair degree of fitness is required to perform some of the combinations. Push-ups are a good way for both partners to gain strength and control.

THE LINDYHOP

1   2   3   4

5   6   7   8

SWING TURN

1

2

3

4

OUT IN TURN

1

2

3

4

ARMS CROSSED PULL OUT

1   2   3   4

HALF TURN ROLL OVER BACK

1   2   3   4

JUMP ON TO HIPS AND THROW

1

2

3

4

SLIDE THROUGH LEGS

1

2

3

4

The Stroll

The Stroll is one of the line dances which has been popular since the late 1950s. Couples face each other, forming two lines. The girls are on one side, the men on the other. These instructions are for the girl. They are the same for the boy, using the left leg instead.

Cross right leg and foot in front of left leg (1). Return it (2).

Repeat action with right leg (3, 4).

Cross right leg and foot behind left leg (5). Return right leg to right side, further to the right than before, so that legs are in open position (6).

Move right leg across in front of left leg (7). Move left leg round behind right leg and close feet together (8).

This is repeated over and over again. Every eight beats the dancers move up one place, and the couple at the top begin to move down the centre aisle (1, 2, 3 and 4 below).

1

5

1

2

3

4

146

2

3

4

6

7

8

The Twist

This dance was one of the first which people performed independently without holding on to each other. However, couples usually face each other, at least to start with. Dancers change direction by stepping out at different angles each time the step is repeated.

The focal point of the Twist is the rotation of the hips. Before attempting the dance, it's a good idea to get the basic feeling of it. This can be done by standing with legs slightly apart, feet facing forwards. Without moving feet, bend first one knee, then the other. As you bend knee, sway hips and transfer weight to straight leg. It is a kind of walking on the spot movement with the hip movements exaggerated. Once you can do this, you're ready to twist.

Both place right foot in front of left. Man bends forward with weight on right foot, girl bends back with weight on left foot, and both sway hips to each side (1, 2).
Man bends back with weight on left foot, girl bends forward with weight on right foot, and both sway hips to each side (3, 4).
Repeat movement (5, 6, 7, 8).

You can vary the dance by twisting when standing upright with weight on both feet, between bending forward and back. The more exaggeratedly you rotate the hips, the better the Twist, especially as Twist music is usually pretty fast.

Another dance you can do to fast Twist music is the Shimmy (9) – you just stand still and shake everything!

1

6

5

148

2

3

4

THE SHIMMY

7

8

9

149

The Frug

The Frug couldn't be simpler. It is literally a step in any direction – forward, back or sideways, on one foot (1), tap with the other (2), a step on the second foot (3) and a tap with the first (4). This is repeated over and over again. Sometimes dancers don't even lift their feet from the ground – they simply change the weight from foot to foot, leaving their feet in place.

For every step and tap there is a movement of the hips forward and back on the off-beat (*and* one *and* two, etc.). This gives the dance a kind of bounce.

There are several possible variations of the Frug:

If you add a jerky rotation of arms, it becomes the Jerk.

If you swing your arms straight up and down in front of you, it becomes the Monkey.

If you extend your thumb upwards, it becomes the Hitchhiker.

If you do the step, tap and step, lifting your knees and using your hands, as if holding reins, it becomes the Pony (see overleaf).

If you mime the breast stroke with your arms, it becomes the Swim (see overleaf).

1

2

3

4

THE JERK

1

2

3

THE MONKEY

1

2

3

4

THE HITCHHIKER

4

1

2

151

THE PONY

1

2

3

4

THE SWIM

1

2

3

4

The Bump

As its name implies, the Bump is a dance in which partners push or bounce off each other. Footwork is not important. Different parts of the body, usually hips and bottoms, are bumped together in time to the music. The Bump takes place on the *off* beat (one *and* two *and* . . .). Six different types of Bump are illustrated here.

The Hustle

The Hustle is the disco dance which, in the form used by couples, most resembles traditional ballroom dancing. The music is heavily influenced by a Latin American feel, which should be reflected in the style of dancing. The first Hustles were done in lines or rows stretched out across the floor.

Here is the L.A. Hustle, or Bus Stop:
Part One: Starting on either foot, step back three steps (1, 2, 3). Tap (4).
Step forward three steps (5, 6, 7).
Tap (8).
Part Two: Step to one side (1).
Slide your feet together (2).

1 PART ONE   **2**   **3**   **4**

1
PART TWO   **2**   **3**   **4**

1 PART THREE   **2**   **3**   **4**

Repeat (3, 4).
Step to the other side (5).
Slide your feet together (6).
Repeat (7, 8).
Part Three: Jump forward with both feet (1).
Hold (2).
Jump back (3).

Hold (4).
Jump forward (5).
Jump back (6).
Click heels (7).
Repeat (8).

See overleaf for Part Four.

5

6

7

8

5

6

7

8

5

6

7

8

The Hustle

Part Four: Tap one foot forward twice (1, 2). Tap foot back twice (3, 4). Tap foot forward (5). Tap foot back (6). Tap foot to side (7). Swing leg across for quarter turn (8).

A simple partner Hustle can be danced holding hands or in the more formal ballroom dance position. This Hustle can be varied by doing the three walking steps in different directions forward, backward, to either side or diagonally.

PART FOUR

PARTNER HUSTLE

Man taps left foot to side, girl taps right foot to side (1). Both walk three steps, the man forward, the girl back (2, 3, 4).

Man taps right foot to side, girl taps left foot to side (5). Both walk three steps, the man back the girl forward (6, 7, 8).